Market and Sell Books

A My Guide

Market and Sell Books

A My Guide

Rebecca Richmond

and

Claire Pickering

Cambridge, England

First published in Great Britain 2014
Reprinted 2016 by My Guide
The Studio
High Green
Great Shelford
Cambridge CB22 5EG

www.januspublishing.co.uk
www.cambridge-media.com

Copyright © 2014 Rebecca Richmond and Claire Pickering

British Library Cataloguing-in-Publication Data

A catalogue record for this book is available from the British Library

The authors REBECCA RICHMOND and CLAIRE PICKERING assert the moral right to be identified as the authors of this work. All rights reserved. No part of this publication may be reproduced, distributed or transmitted in any form or by any means, including photocopying, recording or other electronic or mechanical methods, without the prior written permission of the publisher, except in the case of brief quotations embodied in critical reviews and certain other non-commercial uses permitted by copyright law. For permission requests, write to the publisher, addressed 'Attention: Permissions Coordinator', at the address above.

Neither the authors nor My Guide accept any responsibility or liability for any loss, damage or injury resulting from the use of any information contained herein.

Book cover image designed by Daniela Frongia, Cais Arts

ISBN-13: 978-1-910141-01-4

Dedication

To all writers who want their books to be read.

Contents

Preface	1
Chapter One – Marketer's Mindset	7
Introduction	7
Why People Buy a Novel	7
Why People Buy Non-Fiction, Self-Help and How-To Books	8
Why Some Books Never Sell	9
Reasons for Not Getting Started	15
Know Your Market	17
Setting a Price for Your Non-Fiction Book	20
Setting a Price for Your Novel	21
Choosing Your Title	21
Choosing Your Cover	25
Endorsements on the Back Cover	27
Compiling a Blurb	28
Compiling Your Author Bio	29
Summary	29
Key Points	30
Next Steps	31
Chapter Two – Using Social Media to Market Your Book	33
Introduction	33
Social Media Marketing	36
Note of Caution – Staying Safe on the Internet	41
Choosing a Moniker	41

Engaging with Your Audience	41
How Much Marketing is Enough?	42
Summary	44
Key Points	44
Next Steps	45
Chapter Three – Facebook	**47**
Introduction	47
Setting Up a Facebook Account	48
Driving Sales with Facebook	52
Timelines	53
Apps	55
About Section	56
Admin Panels	57
Engage With Your Audience	57
Ways to Engage	58
Creating a Fan Page	59
Top Tips for Building an Effective Page	60
Things to Avoid	60
Facebook Groups	61
Word of Caution	62
Add a Video	62
Paid Facebook Advertisements	63
Geotargeting for Advertisers	64
Summary	64
Key Points	65
Next Steps	65
Chapter Four – Twitter	**67**
Introduction	67
Setting Up Your Account	69
Twitter Profile	70

Contents

Bios	70
Twitter Header	71
Twitter Background	71
Some Basic Commands	71
Direct Messages	72
Hashtags	73
Twitter Abbreviations	75
Finding Influential Followers	77
The Best Way to Get Followers	78
Driving Sales with Twitter	79
Limitations	79
Getting Past the Twitter Barrier	80
Guidelines for Tweeting	81
Things to Tweet About	82
Paid Advertising on Twitter	84
Things to Avoid	85
Things to Do	85
Using SocialOomph to Automate Twitter	85
Creating an Extended Profile in SocialOomph	86
How to Schedule Posts in Advance on SocialOomph	86
Summary	88
Key Points	89
Next Steps	90
Chapter Five – LinkedIn, YouTube and Pinterest	93
Introduction	93
LinkedIn	94
Creating a LinkedIn Account	95
Driving Sales with LinkedIn	96
LinkedIn Groups	97

LinkedIn Tips	99
Things to Avoid When Using LinkedIn	99
LinkedIn Status Updates	101
LinkedIn Company Pages	102
Creating a LinkedIn Company Page	102
Establishing Your Own LinkedIn Group	104
Getting Started	105
Difference Between Endorsements and Recommendations	106
YouTube	107
Creating a YouTube Account	107
Making an Effective Video	109
Driving Sales with YouTube	110
Pinterest	111
Setting Up a Pinterest Account	112
Adding Pins to Your Boards	113
Adding Products to Your Boards	113
Copyright and Pinterest	114
Driving Sales with Pinterest	114
Sourcing More Ideas for Pins	115
Summary	117
Key Points	117
Next Steps	118
Chapter Six – Websites	**121**
Introduction	121
Custom-Built Websites	122
Selling Through Your Site	123
Domain Names	123
Website Content	125
How to Use a Website to Your Advantage	126

Contents

Using a Website to Market Non-Fiction/Self-Help Books	127
Using a Website to Market Fiction Books	128
Search Engine Optimization (SEO)	129
Login Pages	130
Shortening URLs	130
Meta Tags	130
RSS (Really Simple Syndication)	132
Google Overview	133
Paid Advertising on Google	134
Google Plus (+)	134
Google Options	135
Summary	136
Key Points	136
Next Steps	137
Chapter Seven – Blogging and Articles	**139**
Introduction	139
What is Blogging?	139
Important Points About Blogging	141
Guest Blogging	144
Articles	145
Online Articles and Keywords	146
Articles and Accuracy	147
Short Stories	148
Sourcing Ideas for Articles and Short Stories Externally	148
Libel and Slander	150
Bias	151
Copyright	151
Images	153

Permissions	153
Plagiarism	153
Summary	154
Key Points	154
Next Step	155
Chapter Eight – Other Marketing Techniques and Tools	**157**
Introduction	157
Marketing Basics	157
Making the Most of Marketing Strategies & Sales Opportunities	158
Creating a Display	159
Sourcing Marketing/Promotional Material	160
Preparing for Public Speaking	160
Don't Expect Perfection	161
Accept Your Nervousness	161
Avoid Trying to be Word Perfect	161
Keep it in Perspective	161
Preparing a Press Release	163
Compiling a Press Release	165
Scribd	166
Advantages of Promoting Your Work on Scribd	166
Opening a Scribd Account	167
GoodReads	169
The Importance of Book Reviews	172
Skype	173
Summary	174
Key Points	175
Next Steps	175

Contents

Chapter Nine – Distribution Outlets   177

  Introduction   177
    Nielsens   177
      ISBN Numbers   177
      Nielsens PubWeb   178
      ISBN Numbers for eBooks   179
      Barcoding   180
    Gardners Books   180
    Amazon   182
      Amazon Advantage Account   184
      Amazon's Author Central   184
      Amazon's Author Pages   184
      Creating an Author Page URL   185
      Amazon Authorgraph   186
      Search Inside the Book With Amazon   186
      Amazon's Listmania!   186
      Amazon Ranking   187
    Kindle   188
      KDP Select   188
  Summary   190
  Key Points   190
  Next Steps   191

Chapter Ten – Organisation and Planning   193

  Introduction   193
  Goals   193
  Planning   195
  Declutter Your Environment   199
  When to do Your Marketing   200
  Where to Work   201

Perseverance	201
Done for the Day?	202
What Qualifies a Book to Become a Bestseller?	203
Summary	204
Key Points	205
Next Steps	205
Final Note From the Authors	207
Index	209
Glossary	215
About the Authors	219
Other Books in the Series	221

Preface

A journey of a thousand miles begins with a single step.

Confucius

Congratulations! In buying this guide you have taken the first steps towards becoming a book marketer. By the very fact that you are accepting responsibility for the success of your book you are already way ahead of many authors. Generally, the number of sales made and the money earned from a book is a reflection of the amount of proactive marketing carried out either by the publisher, the author or both.

- ☺ You don't need to be an experienced sales person or Internet marketer to achieve book sales. In fact, the good news is that a large majority of your marketing can be done by writing and utilising the immense power of the Internet and social media – which we assume you enjoy since you're a writer.

If you cringe at the thought of selling, this book is for you. As authors ourselves, we are not naturally gifted at marketing and neither of us would ever have chosen a career in sales. However, we believe our books can really help people and therefore, we have realised that by not telling the world about them, we are denying people the opportunity to use the information they contain to live happier lives.

If you have written a novel it might not be life-changing, but if you truly believe it is well written and an enjoyable read, why would you keep it to yourself? We are all generally happy to recommend a great movie or a restaurant we think family or friends will enjoy and recommending your book to people you engage with via social media and blogs is much the same – except you are the author.

Our methods are simple yet effective. Rebecca's first self-help book – designed to help people manage the symptoms of the debilitating illness of fibromyalgia – was read by people in ten countries within just four days of its release, and this was achieved using methods within this guide.

Marketing your book effectively can help you to:

- achieve fame, as writing a book is often a good way to establish celebrity status
- become recognised and respected as an expert in your field
- earn an income
- increase your credibility and visibility
- gain a competitive edge
- learn new skills
- leave a legacy
- help people change and improve their lives
- share your expertise with a wider audience
- spread an idea
- express yourself as a creative writer
- bring pleasure to people's lives through your stories.

Although very few authors sell enough books each year to make a living solely from writing, once you are a published author it can lead to additional income from various sources, such as new business, commanding higher fees, upselling higher-priced products and services, speaking engagements, interviews and joint ventures. You can also capitalise on your asset by making your book available in additional formats: audio, electronic, etc.

Typing 'The End' is only the beginning. Even if you feel you have written the next bestseller, you will first have to attract readers. This guide has been written specifically to help you market your book, which means leveraging your author platform, and increasing visibility and exposure. These are all words that you will see an increasing amount of as you start to use social media to market your book, in what is clearly not a passing phase or a fad, with new social media platforms developing all the time.

Sadly, the quality of your book does not guarantee that it will sell thousands of copies. Even if you spend thousands on marketing and invest an equal amount in hours, you cannot force people to buy it and physically part with their hard-earned cash. It is not just a question of uploading your book onto Amazon and then waiting for the sales to come rolling in. So what exactly is marketing?

Marketing is essentially the process of telling people about your book in order to get it noticed, raise its profile and generate sales. In essence, it is about gaining the attention of potential readers. Free publicity is great and if you are able to secure interviews or reviews, you should welcome the opportunity. But be careful to ensure that the interview reflects the image you want to achieve for your book and that it is not exploited. If you pay for your publicity in the form of advertisements in magazines, newspapers and on the radio, etc., you have more control, but it can be expensive and therefore, in this book we are putting most of our focus on free and low-cost advertising.

> *For a business not to advertise is like winking at a girl in the dark. You know what you are doing but no one else does.*
>
> Stuart H. Britt

Whilst it may be very tempting to start your next book, if you do that you need to be realistic about whether or not you will have time to market the one you have already written.

- ☺ Use every available opportunity to market your work and in fact, 90 per cent of your time should be spent marketing, as time spent marketing equals sales.

Because of our society's obsession with celebrities, books written by people in the public eye have an almost guaranteed market for sales. But, assuming you are not a celebrity, you will need to generate interest in you, your subject and what you have to say.

Some authors are determined to find a publisher or an agent and mistakenly believe they won't need to do any marketing. But even if you have secured a publisher, the company may not have the resources available to undertake sufficient marketing to maximise sales. It should be a two-way partnership between yourself and the publisher because, generally, promoting your book is about engaging with the general public – the readers – and that is most effectively done by you. After all, you both have one common objective: to make as many sales as possible, thereby earning you both an income.

It is never too early to start marketing. If you begin marketing before your book is finished, you will be able to build up interest in your book launch and hopefully generate immediate sales. Proactively marketing your book before it is finished can also help you obtain a publishing deal, as publishers and agents will almost certainly ascertain whether or not you are able to market or promote your book.

The Internet is now an integral part of our daily lives and it is hard to imagine life without it, with connection speeds increasing all the time. In fact, the Internet is no longer a luxury but a necessity, with the use of smartphones and apps becoming commonplace.

Blogging and writing articles and short stories is the fastest way to share your material with millions of people across the globe, allowing you to become an international author. We still find it amazing when we receive emails from people on the other side of the world praising our books or articles. Without the Internet, it would have been incredibly difficult for us to reach such a wide audience.

With over a million books published every year, these days it is much harder to get a book noticed. How well you market your book can literally mean the difference between success and failure in terms of sales. Our aim is to make the steps you need to take as simple as possible in order for you to begin marketing successfully.

There are so many social media platforms that it would be impossible for us to focus on all of them, not to mention that it would be overwhelming for you. Therefore, we have devoted complete chapters to Facebook, Twitter and blogging, as these are our favourite methods of using social media to market a book. As well as being the most popular, we believe they are the most effective.

As published authors of several self-help books, we take particular interest in nurturing the new talent of writers of fiction and non-fiction, so both are covered in this book. Although the marketing methods are very similar, where there are slight variations required we have made this clear in the text.

Preface

One of the best ways to learn is from other people's mistakes – and we have made quite a few. One of the most valuable lessons we have learnt is that successful marketing is not simply a case of working hard – it is essential to work effectively. Whether you choose you use this guide to brush up your skills in certain areas or diligently work through each chapter, utilising the information we are sharing can help you to formulate a targeted marketing campaign, potentially saving you months of wasted effort, so let's get started ...

The way to get started is to quit talking and begin doing.
Walt Disney

Chapter One – Marketer's Mindset

The difference between perseverance and obstinacy is that one comes from a strong will, and the other from a strong won't.

Henry Ward Beecher

Introduction

A marketer's mindset is very different to that of a writer's and it requires different skills. Fortunately, technology these days means you can utilise your writing skills to market your book. Whilst it would be great if you could let others take care of the marketing for you and let the sales come pouring in, in reality it doesn't happen that way.

Why People Buy a Novel

You might think the obvious answers include the following:

- The book is compelling and/or entertaining.
- Readers believe it will transport them to another world for a while, bringing relief from everyday hassles, dramas, stresses and problems.

While people may want the above from a book, they have no way of knowing if your particular book will meet this criteria until they are actually reading. There are an infinite number of reasons why someone will choose a particular novel, including some of the following:

- The author is a celebrity.
- It has a great opening paragraph or first page (this is usually about as much as they will read in the shop or online before making a purchase).
- They have read and enjoyed other titles by the same author.

- Word of mouth, in as much as friends and relatives are talking about and recommending a book they have read.
- The cover, title or blurb appealed to them as they were browsing.
- It has been reviewed and recommended by a magazine, newspaper or TV show they enjoy.
- They saw or heard the author being interviewed and it sparked their interest.
- It is appearing on a bestsellers list.
- They watched the film or TV show first.

Why People Buy Non-Fiction, Self-Help and How-To Books

There are lots of reasons people may buy a non-fiction title, some of the most common being:

- They believe it will solve a problem they have.
- They hope it will improve their lives or help them achieve a goal, such as earning more money, finding love, losing weight, etc.
- It has a niche market and they are seeking specialist information on a topic in which they have great interest.

The reason they will choose a particular book above all the others covering the same topic include some of the following:

- The author is a celebrity.
- It contains unique information that is current, in demand and cannot be found elsewhere.
- The author is regarded as an authority in their field.
- Something in the blurb or the author's bio leads them to believe that the author knows what they are talking about and perhaps has overcome that particular problem themselves.
- The foreword gives them confidence that they will gain the knowledge they seek.
- It is part of a series, like the *My Guide* series of self-help books, where the reader has enjoyed other books in the series.

- It has great endorsements.
- It is on the bestsellers list.
- The contents page appears to cover the aspects they are interested in.
- Word of mouth, in as much as friends and relatives are talking about and recommending a book they have read.

Think about it – if a hairdresser or shopkeeper recommended a book they had read to several different people they encountered each day, a book title can be promoted very easily.

With the Internet, word of mouth is no longer the only means of promoting a book. Instead of recommendations or a book just being passed between close friends, it can now reach across the world in a very short time. In other words, it can go viral. This is a term used when lots of other people are retweeting, reposting or repinning your material. In other words, forwarding emails, images or videos to their own followers that have amused, informed or intrigued them. The influence of this type of marketing, brand awareness and its influence on sales is enormous. The book *The Secret* by Rhonda Byrne achieved great success as people began talking about the changes they had made in their lives after reading it and it has sold millions of copies.

Why Some Books Never Sell

It may be that despite plugging your book and coming up with marketing strategies, your book still doesn't sell more than a handful of copies. This can be for several reasons:

- saturated genre
- inappropriate overall page count (where the book is too long or short)
- perceived as over-priced
- uninteresting book title
- poor layout and formatting
- weak first sentence, paragraph, page or foreword
- uninteresting subject matter
- not user-friendly enough
- inadequate marketing
- badly written/poor content

- bad reviews
- poor or non-existent editing
- market too small
- corners cut on production.

If you have not already completed your book, it would be worth investing time in ensuring your book is marketable and identifying your target audience before you go any further. In other words, stop and ask yourself: Who is the book for? However, if you have already written your book then the same question is equally important in order to enable you to market it effectively.

Think about your book and why someone would want to buy it. This means going deeper than simply saying 'they would enjoy it'. If it is non-fiction, answering the following questions is a great start:

1. Non-fiction

If you have written a non-fiction book, consider:
- Does it solve a problem for them?
- What will they gain by reading your book?
- Is it user-friendly and easy to read?
- Is your book good value/is the price competitive?
- Is the content unique?
- Will the information help them achieve a goal?
- Does it offer a new take on a topic?
- What books already published are you in competition with?
- Why is your book different to others already on the market?
- What qualifies you to write this book?
- What key message do you wish to communicate?

2. Fiction

- What genre is your book?
- What books already published are you in competition with?

- Why is your book different to other books already on the market?
- Is your book similar to another very successful book?
- What emotions do I expect my novel to evoke in its readers?

If your book is similar to another already on the market, readers of that book might want to read your book as well. For example, when a book has been very successful there are lots of similar books published, hoping to ride on the success of the first book. Good examples of this are the *Harry Potter* series, *Bridget Jones's Diary* and *Fifty Shades of Grey*. There is nothing wrong with this strategy and it can be highly successful, as long as you don't plagiarise the content.

Most people find marketing a book a scary prospect and many excuses are given for not actually getting started – arguments for this being:

- I haven't got the time.
- I don't know where to start.
- It will probably be too expensive.
- I don't like technology and it will be too difficult.
- Using social media will result in losing my privacy.

This is a negative attitude and will definitely hinder you in getting your work out there. As Henry Ford famously said: 'Whether you think you can or you think you can't, you're probably right'.

It is common to begin with great gusto and enthusiasm, plunging in, getting caught up in the excitement, then running into problems at some point and backing off or even abandoning book marketing altogether. The important thing to remember is that you are not alone – stumbling blocks are commonplace. However, the difference between you and other people is that you have the benefit of this guide behind you, helping you to avoid the usual pitfalls.

> *If you can find a path with no obstacles, it probably doesn't lead anywhere.*
>
> *Frank A. Clark*

Coaching Tip:

Don't try to do everything yourself. Try to outsource things. Remove blockages to your success. Analyse what is holding you back and what you are finding you haven't got time to do.

Think of it as an equation:

Time spent direct selling plus time spent indirect selling equals copies sold.

Before you begin marketing your book, you need to develop a publicist's mindset. It is not enough to say you want to make money or sell your book. Everyone wants those things, but not everyone can achieve those goals – it takes a certain mindset.

☺ Thankfully, it does not mean you need to be a workaholic, engage in questionable marketing tactics or become a pushy, overbearing salesperson who people run away from to avoid.

The secret behind adopting a successful marketing is to follow the PIP formula: Perseverance, Integrity and Planning:

1. Perseverance

Positive perseverance is crucial. Accept now that you are going to have down times. Something will go wrong at some point and you need to be able to move on from it or find a way around the problem.

Successful people in all walks of life display unshakeable persistence. More than 2,000 years ago Confucius said: 'Our greatest glory is not in never failing but in rising every time we fall.' How much you are prepared to persevere will depend greatly on how much you want the end result. One of the crucial factors in getting the result you want is to focus on your end goal rather than the steps you would have to do to get there. For example, if you focus on having to spend four hours a day on marketing activities, it is not going to motivate you in the same way as focusing on selling 50,000 copies or the royalty payment in your bank account.

Having a goal that is too far away or too big can also be demotivating. So give yourself smaller goals that you can achieve and celebrate along the way, to keep yourself motivated.

2. Integrity

We cannot overstress the importance of believing in your book. The dictionary definition of 'integrity' is 'the quality of being honest and having strong moral principles'. If you do not believe it will provide an entertaining read, adequate information or help people overcome the problems it claims to, how can you possibly sell with confidence? However, if you genuinely believe that your book is a great product – and that it does what it says on the tin, so to speak – why would you have any worries about selling it?

> *A bend in the road is not the end of the road ... unless you fail to make the turn.*
>
> *Helen Keller*

Many authors are uncomfortable selling. But let me ask you a simple question: if you had a friend who was suffering from a terrible headache or hayfever and you knew of something you truly believed would help them, would you feel bad recommending it? If you believe in your book, then surely telling people who need the information it supplies is being kind and helpful ...

☺ Simply think about it as recommending a great restaurant.

Marketing is not about pushing your book to everyone you meet – it is about seeking out people who may benefit from or enjoy the information it provides and simply telling them how they can obtain it.

☺ I am not a natural salesperson, but I was once told by the CEO of one of the world's leading sports brands that I should have been in sales. This was because I passionately believed that what I was saying was correct.

When I started to sell my own books, my natural shyness and lack of confidence kicked in – that is, until I accepted that I was acting with integrity. I was not stating that my books would change the world, but simply that my belief was that the information contained in my books would help people with a similar problem or goal if they used it correctly.

So what are you choosing to accept as your core belief to help you develop the marketer's mindset? To get you thinking in the right way, start by finishing this sentence: I believe the information in my book will …

☺ Note: it is a belief and therefore personal to you and no one can dispute it.

Remember, there is nothing more off-putting than someone who appears desperate to sell *any* product, including a book. By seeking out people who may be interested in your content or genre, you can tell them it is available without accosting everyone you meet. While you may miss the occasional opportunity to sell a copy, in the long run the more reserved approach will pay off.

3. Planning

> *A clear vision, backed by definite plans, gives you a tremendous feeling of confidence and personal power.*
>
> Brian Tracy

Fail to plan – plan to fail! The more meticulous you are with your plans, the greater control you will have, thereby increasing your confidence and success. To become an authority on your topic or to become recognised as an author of a particular genre, you need to portray your confidence in your book and other products you may wish to upsell.

As we explain the marketing processes, you can develop your plan and test which methods best suit your personality and lifestyle. You can then monitor results so you can make an informed choice as to which marketing strategies work best for you.

It is pointless planning to be on ten different social media platforms for four hours a day, if you are working full time, managing a family or have other commitments. Making sensible plans focused on your end goal, measuring success along the way, will help ensure you stay on the right track; this will be covered in more detail later.

☺ Be realistic about the timescales within which you expect to achieve your goals. If you only attain 90 per cent of them, instead of beating yourself up about the missed 10 per cent, celebrate your successes and look at what you did right. See how it can be improved and repeat the process to achieve the remainder of your goal.

Reasons for Not Getting Started

There are many reasons people give for not getting started, especially if it is something they don't want to do, if it is something new or if they are unsure what they are doing. Some of the most common excuses include:

1. Overwhelm

When you try to do too many things at once it is easy to become overwhelmed. It is also difficult to give each area sufficient focus. This is why we have focused our attention on the ones we believe will give you the best start when marketing your book.

2. Fear of the Unknown

The chances are that this is new experience for you and it is natural to feel apprehensive. Perhaps you are a technophobe who quakes at thought of engaging with people over the Internet. Or maybe the idea of public speaking is terrifying for you. But if you:

- plan and measure results
- choose the techniques that best suit your personality and lifestyle
- take things at your own pace
- learn each platform fully before introducing another

then with time and each success, your confidence will grow.

3. People Won't Like Me

We are sorry but you are right, some people won't like you and will probably be critical or even nasty about you, your book and your work. It is said that approximately 30 per cent of people you meet won't like you and that the more successful you become, the more polarised opinion will be. It may be the way you speak, look, hold yourself, behave or simply the colour of your hair.

The first thing to do is accept that you cannot please everyone. Don't dilute your opinions so they become bland and wishy-washy. Some very successful people have become so by deliberately having very strong views or by writing fiction in an unusual style. What they have done is create a 'Marmite' effect, whereby people either love them or hate them – the upside of this being that the people who love them avidly read everything they write.

People have their own issues and beliefs that affect their judgement of you. By sticking to your beliefs and maintaining your integrity, you will find it much easier to rise above any nasty comments. Remember – it is only one person's opinion, whose opinion you may not even value, anyway. You could always choose to view it as useful, constructive feedback or criticism, thereby turning it into a positive.

☺ Remember – no publicity is bad publicity.

4. Fear of Failure

If you are concerned about putting 100 per cent into your marketing and still achieving only limited sales, this could put you off before you even get started. There are two main reasons many people fear failure:

- looking foolish in front of others
- feeling bad about themselves.

Of course we understand these concerns, but if you have written a book and don't make any sales because you haven't bothered to market it, that can also be seen as failure. So it is better to have tried and failed than not to have tried at all – or is that love? ☺

Acknowledge the fact that you are a publicist, marketer, PR consultant, salesperson or whatever title it is that you want to give yourself. For many people, the fear of failure is greatly reduced if no one knows about it, so they avoid telling people that they are self-promoting their work.

> **Coaching Tip:**
>
> Be brave – put yourself on the line. If you haven't told anybody yet that you are studying this guide and intend to actively promote your book, get out there and start telling people. Ideally, share goals you set around marketing your book with at least one person. If possible, choose three people – a friend, colleague or family member – and tell them what you are doing.
>
> Why would we put you through this? Well, it is quite simple, really. As we all know, it is easy to procrastinate and tell yourself you will get round to promoting your book next week or month. But when we tell someone

we are going to do something, we automatically feel committed and are more likely to take action.

But don't pick people who you know will be critical and put you under pressure, or ones who are going to let you off the hook too easily. Choose positive people, who will encourage you and be supportive of your goals.

Know Your Market

If you haven't already done so, you need to consider what type of person your target reader is. Far too often authors believe their book will appeal to everyone. Because this is highly unlikely, in this chapter we will be helping you to identify your target audience and use your marketer's mindset to locate them.

Even more than the quality of a book, its potential for success relies on there being sufficient people with an interest in the subject. But with your ability to identify, locate and engage with your target market, any book has the potential to be successful.

A self-help book such as *My Guide: Manage Fibromyalgia/CFS* cannot be classified as general market. However, it relates to a distressing condition affecting approximately 3 per cent of the population, for which there is currently little help available. When you consider that the world's population is nearly 7 billion, that equates to a possible 210 million people suffering from this condition, thereby making it a marketable commodity with potentially huge sales.

First, get yourself a large piece of paper and a pen and brainstorm the following:

1. Who is your book written for/who is your ideal customer?
    - females/males
    - young adults/children
    - married/single
    - parents
    - employed/unemployed
    - housewives/husbands
    - students
    - senior citizens

2. What is their pain, problem, concern, opportunity?
3. Are they overweight?
4. Are they looking to change career?
5. Do they want to be better parents?
6. Are they trying to get pregnant?
7. Are they looking for certain types of information? For example, if you have identified that your target readers are overweight housewives, are they:
   - Looking to lose weight?
   - Wanting to find out how to dress to flatter their fuller figure?
   - Wanting to increase their confidence and self-esteem?
   - Looking for career opportunities in modelling for plus-size models?
8. Next, look at where to locate them and how to talk so they will listen.
9. Where do they live?
10. Do they have children?
11. What is their income bracket?
12. What programmes do they watch or listen to?
13. What do they read?
14. Are they using any forums or support groups on the Internet?
15. Do they have any hobbies or interests?
16. If they read newspapers or magazines, what type do they buy?
17. Where and how do they spend their spare time?
18. What language do they speak?
19. Where do they shop?
20. Are there any words or terms of speech that will resonate with them?

Continue listing even small details until you have amassed as much information as you can. Obviously, there will always be exceptions to every rule.

- ☺ However, if you have written a book on how to lose weight for your wedding, it is unlikely that your readers will be 78-year-old retired male builders from the Outer Hebrides – but you never know.

By having a clear picture of who is most likely to buy your book, you can target your market. This process is particularly important if you are hoping to sell them further products or services on the back of your book, known as upselling.

We understand that not all subjects will be as easy to break down. For example if you have written a book on how to overcome insomnia, this is a problem that can apply to both male and female audiences, of all age groups. However, it generally affects more women than men and often the problem increases between the ages of 30 and 40. Whilst I would not want to exclude 30-year-old males from my marketing campaign, I would keep in mind that their concerns around lack of sleep differ somewhat from those of ladies suffering from the same problem.

Likewise, fantasy or romance novels won't appeal to everyone. However, stereotypes don't always apply, as there is nothing to say that women can't be interested in thrillers and men in historical romance, and vice versa.

Secondly, you will need to study your competition and see if you can learn from them. For example:

- How do they go about marketing their book/s?
- What do they do that seems to work well?
- Can you learn anything from them?
- What tips can you take away?

You should analyse your followers regularly and ensure that the content is relevant to them. In other words, you wouldn't post something about having a baby on a pensioners' site and likewise, young adults wouldn't necessarily be interested in bridge or bowls contests. Make your posts relevant to your audience and perhaps target them via email.

☺ According to Gary Vaynerchuk's book *Crush It!*, the best question you can ever ask on social media is, 'What can I do for you?'

Setting a Price for Your Non-Fiction Book

If you are working with a publisher, they may well want to dictate the price of your book. When determining a recommended retail price it is not a decision to be taken lightly, as it is an important marketing tool. If you are able to influence the price, don't be fooled into thinking that the cheaper it is, the more you can sell, as in certain markets a low price would indicate inferior quality. For example, if you were offered a diamond ring for £10 or fillet steak at 10p/kg, you could be forgiven for thinking there was something not quite right.

Think – PRICE:

P – Problem, Pain or Passion

Is the content of your book going to help the reader deal with a problem that is causing them a lot of pain? Is it a subject that invokes a great deal of passion in a niche market? The greater the pain and the passion, the more likely it is that people will be willing to pay for the information in your book.

R – Relevance

How relevant is your content? Be honest with yourself. Overpricing your book could limit sales and it is better to sell a million books at £1, than sell 100 at £30.

I – Intention

If you intend to use the book as a way to market your services to potential customers, you may wish to consider selling it at a much lower price in order to introduce them to your skills, experience and knowledge.

C – Competition

Look at how much competition there is in your chosen subject or genre. If the market is saturated with books by well-known authors that are already selling well, you may need to discount your book in order to break into the market.

E – Exclusivity

Is the information in your book available elsewhere? Is it easy to obtain from other sources? My book, *My Guide: Manage Fibromyalgia/CFS*, detailed the techniques I used to recover from the condition. As I am one of only a handful of people who has developed their own recovery programme and there is no recognised cure, I was confident that the information was not readily available elsewhere. There may be 1,000 books on a subject, meaning that there is lots of competition, but you may have unique information.

Setting a Price for Your Novel

Novels generally command a lower price than non-fiction books. This is because the readers are looking for enjoyment as opposed to potentially life-changing information. Therefore, it is important to market your book at a competitive price.

If you are an unknown author, people will be unwilling to pay significantly more for your book than they would for a similar novel. Only the most popular authors can command a premium for their much-awaited books.

The next thing to consider is printing and publishing costs, as unless you have sufficient financial means to cover any losses, you need to ensure your costs are covered.

Publishing your book as an eBook gives you the chance to test the market before investing in the more costly business of publishing a printed version. Obviously there is less profit to be made from an eBook sold at 99 pence, but it could also allow you to sell some books, obtain reviews and then later increase your price once you have established your book in the marketplace. And from a reader's perspective, what have you got to lose if you have paid such a small amount for a book?

Choosing Your Title

We are assuming you are at the stage where you have already chosen a great title for your book, but just in case you are getting ahead of the game and starting your marketing before your book goes to print, we thought we would share with you some valuable information on choosing the right title.

In just a few words, your title needs to capture your reader's imagination and give them a strong indication as to the topic. A good title is essential for two reasons: it will catch the potential buyer's eye on the shelf in a bookshop and it will appear on the searches of online bookstores like Amazon. Coming up with a title that does both these important jobs can be challenging, but it is well worth investing the time to get it right.

In the first place, it needs to be catchy and to hook people. Consider whether or not it is something that can be serialised, such as the *Chicken Soup* series by Mark Victor Hansen and Jack Canfield. The *Chicken Soup* books have over 100 titles, one of these being *Chicken Soup for the Soul*. An example of a serialised novel would be *Harry Potter* by J. K. Rowling or *The Green Mile* by Stephen King, which was originally published in six-monthly instalments in 1996 and was later released as a single volume in May 1997. A famous example would be Charles Dickens' *Pickwick Papers*, which became a household name.

Another widely recognised and well-researched title is *The Secret* by Rhonda Byrne. Consider having more than one-word titles, which can limit search results. Yes, we know this example is just one word (excluding the word 'the') and it does not describe what the book is about, but it was excellently marketed and was brought out after a DVD of the same name. The title of this book is very clever in that you automatically want to know what the secret is.

The problem with one-word titles is that it can limit search results. For instance, if your book was called *Eden* and someone searched for this on the Internet, they would more than likely come up with The Eden Project, thereby missing out on valuable sales. Whereas a title such as *The Mists of Eden*, which is more specific, would bring up results for just this book title and so aids potential sales.

When researching your title, check whether or not other authors have used the same title, so that you don't become associated by default with their work. This can work in both the positive and the negative, in that a book with the same title as you that receives a good or a bad review can be connected mistakenly with your manuscript. Have a look at what other titles you are competing with.

Grab a pen and some paper and jot down words that spring to mind as you review the following list. If possible, it should:

- tell them what it is about at a glance
- have a hook and create an intrigue, so they want to know more
- deliver what it says on the tin

- be something that can be serialised
- raise curiosity and spark interest
- contain the words your would-be buyers will type into Google or Amazon, or other such sites, to assist with marketing.

When we were choosing the title for our book, *My Guide: How to Write a Novel*, we first researched our market and looked at what people were searching for. Having determined that the words 'write' and 'novel' needed to be in the title, we had a base from which to start. Initially, we came up with an extensive list before settling on one:

Writing a Novel Made Simple

Write a Novel: Unlock/Unleash the Author Within

How to Write a Novel: The Course That's Not a Course

How to Write a Novel – Step-by-Step Guide

How to Write a Novel People Will Want to Read Teach Yourself How to Write a Great Novel

When I Grow Up, I Want to be a Writer (limited search results)

When I Grow Up, I Want to Write a Book (limited search results)

The Novelty of Writing (play on word 'novel')

Anyone Can Write a Book

You Can Write Your Own Book

Write Your Own Story

Secrets of Writing a Novel (though not really a secret)

Your Chance to Write a Novel

A Book, By You

Become an Author

Write a Book with Our Helpful Guide

Tell a Story

Write a Novel in Your Own Time

The Novelist's Bible (decided against this as it has religious associations, maybe restricting readership)

Your Own Little Blueprint

Novelist's Blueprint

Share Your Story

Your Chance to Share Your Story

The Myth of Writing a Novel (decided against this as not really a myth)

The Key to Being a Novelist What Makes a Good Novelist

Unleash the Author Within Novels, Writing and You

Your Story, Your Keyboard, From Home/Wherever

Homemade Novel

Grow a Novel (this is a title that can be serialised)

Everyone's Got it in Them

Cultivating a Novelist (limited search results)

Teach Yourself

Home-grown Novelist (limited search results)

Practical Guide to Writing a Novel

Writing a Novel Demystified

The Mystery of Writing a Novel Unravelled

Mythbusters: How to Write a Novel

Easyish Guides ...

Simplish/Simplistic Guides ...

Chapter and Verse (again has religious connotations)

Writing a Novel in 12 Easy Steps (referring to the number of chapters)

Ingredients to Writing a Novel

Idiot's Guide to Writing a Novel (too similar to existing title)

Write a Novel Made Easy

Writing a Novel Made Easy

Write a Novel: Steps 1, 2, 3

Insider's Guide to Writing a Novel

A–Z of Writing a Novel

Recipe for Successful Novel Writing (not a recipe; limited search results unless know exact title)

As you can see from this list, smaller words such as prepositions and conjunctions do not take a capital letter. We had great fun compiling this list and a lot of laughs playing around with words as one title led to another idea before finally settling on one – *My Guide: How to Write a Novel* – the idea being that we could have a *My Guide* series.

Choosing Your Cover

To coin a well-oiled phrase, like it or not, people do judge a book by its cover and in addition to the title, this is the first thing people will see. It therefore needs to be something that will attract attention and thereby potential readers.

Covers, otherwise known as jackets, were originally designed to protect the pages within and to stop them from falling out. They have now become an essential part of promoting a book. Years ago, leather-bound books were more statements about the owner than the contents of the book. All sorts of selling tools have been used over the years when designing book covers, including stamped and embossed scenes, which were introduced in the 1870s and 80s.

A well-designed cover can encourage a reader to pick up a book in the first place, so it is important to consider many aspects when designing one. Cover designers of successful books have experimented with them over the years, often taking the opportunity to rebrand when it came to new print runs. George Orwell's *1984* sold in its millions and has been assigned over fifteen different cover designs in its sixty years in print. In short, with each new print run the cover was modernised and adapted to reflect fashion trends and changes in society, in order to appeal to alternative markets.

Penguin is recognised for introducing well-known authors to the mass market. Part of their strategy was to denote each genre by adopting a particular typography and colour. The brilliance of this idea was that it made all the books in a particular genre instantly recognisable, thereby appealing to the human desire to collect a full set.

Book covers can offer an interpretation of its contents. Even if you are producing your book as an eBook, the cover still has to look like something worth buying, and perhaps worth keeping. Online, the only distinguishing feature is the cover and with the increase in demand for eBooks, cover design has become even more important.

When choosing or designing a book cover there are all sorts of things that need to be taken into consideration:

- White backgrounds cannot be seen very well in the format of a thumbnail on Internet sites like Amazon. A thumbnail is where your cover image is reduced in size equivalent to that of a small button, similar in dimension to the nail on your thumb.
- If you don't want to employ the services of a designer, there are sites out there such as <http://www.iStockphoto.com> that enable you to download images. Sites like these enable you to create a design of your own by putting several images together, or you can use one of theirs. These images are inexpensive and some are even free; however, sales exceeding a certain limit may incur an additional fee. The downside of using online images is that they are not unique. It is still worth considering though, as the services of graphic artists, illustrators and designers can be costly.
- Consider whether or not you want to serialise your books. For instance, you may want the covers to have a similar layout so that they are easily identifiable on the shelves, making them specific to you as an author or company. In other words, standardising your layout. In our case, for the *My Guide* series we have done this with colours, our 'morph' figure and layout.
- If you have one, do you want your logo to appear both on the spine and on the back cover in a particular position? Also consider positioning if serialising.
- Does your cover represent the contents of the book?
- Does your cover design sell the book, encouraging people to pick it up, rather than repelling them?
- Will your cover design appeal to your target audience?
- Is there a talking point?

When looking at various designs for our own books, it proved to be a big learning curve and we held many brainstorming sessions as we considered many aspects, including:

- If the design could be standardised for the series.

- Whether the design would translate well into other formats – Web headers, posters, banners, etc.
- If the photograph or picture was dark, how would it look on a black background?
- If we chose a red background, how would it look if we had a pink picture, as the two colours might clash?
- If the photograph was pale, it might be lost on a white background – how could we get over this?
- For eBbooks, the cover has to work even in reduced format (thumbnail size). To do this it requires a lot less detail, with more effective colours and very clear fonts of a good size for the title and author name, so they remain legible when reduced.
- Because a book is rectangular in shape, by their very nature their covers don't translate well to a square thumbnail, thereby potentially losing important details from the image.
- Did we want our front cover image duplicated or mirrored on the back cover?
- If we used a photograph and were serialising our books, we needed to consider having some sort of common border to them.
- Was the border shape we had chosen suitable to take most images?

Don't be tempted to take short cuts when designing your book cover, as it can mean the difference between gaining sales and your book remaining undiscovered.

Endorsements on the Back Cover

An endorsement is where a well-respected or well-known individual who has read your book provides a short quote or testimonial about it; in other words, validating it. Often, there is a place on the back of the jacket for this, in addition to the blurb. They can also be placed in the interior preliminary pages of the book. As with reviews, a glowing endorsement from an expert can convince someone to purchase a book.

If you already have endorsements for your book, you should definitely consider displaying the best one or the one from the most reputable source on the back cover of your book. This will add credibility and help increase sales.

Because not many of us know someone famous, endorsements for non-fiction should come from experts in the field in which you have written – those who hold senior roles for organisations known to your target audience, such as CEOs, entrepreneurs, speakers, local personalities, well-known names. You can usually fit two or three endorsements on the back cover. If you have more than this, they can be placed in the preliminary pages of your book. Go for quality rather than quantity; if you secure too many endorsements, you can always save them for a second edition or use them on your website or other promotional material.

For fiction, approaching published authors who write in the same genre as you can be useful. You could also approach magazines, papers, radio shows or Internet sites that review books. If you happen to know someone in the public eye who would be willing to read your book and provide an endorsement, this can be very effective.

Compiling a Blurb

There is a definite art to compiling a compelling blurb for the back cover, summarising what your book is about, and it is by no means as simple as it looks. Ernest Hemingway said: 'There is nothing to writing. All you do is sit down at a typewriter and bleed', whereas marketing and writing a blurb is probably one of the hardest things you will have to do, albeit crucial.

You will have spent many months, perhaps even years, compiling your manuscript and now you are being asked to cut everything out and summarise it in a few words. As a guide, you are looking for around just 250 words. It is your chance to further engage the potential purchaser, grabbing their attention from the outset, unleashing a sense of intrigue. You are the ideal person to do this, in that it is you who knows the book best and its relevant strengths. Failing that, your editor or your publisher can produce one. Have a go using the following guidelines:

- use attention-grabbing words and phrases
- utilise ellipses and question marks, to keep the reader asking questions
- give a hint as to what's inside the cover.
- reviews, quotations, etc., should remain unchanged
- consider words and phrases used by your target audience.

This is the one place where you can use the punctuation marks you are generally told to avoid – such as exclamation marks, en rules, parentheses and ellipses – so have fun using them to great effect, to create intrigue and leave the reader wanting more.

Compiling Your Author Bio

Your author bio will appear either on the back cover of your book or within its interior pages. Wherever it is to appear, your readers will want to know about you, so it is important to decide how much you want to share with them. If your book is non-fiction, your bio should definitely tell them what qualifies you to have written the book. It should therefore include information about your background experience or successes in the field in which you have written. You should also include a couple of sentences of a more personal nature. For example, you might want to tell them you live in Dorset where, when you are not writing, the scenery inspires you to paint.

If your book is a novel, you can share details of how your writing career started. Again, it is helpful to tell them roughly where you live and what you enjoy doing apart from writing – you might be surprised what connects with them.

I always read author bios in the books I read but rarely remember them. However, one that struck a chord with me was Jill Mansell, who shared how she writes 'only when she's completely run out of displacement activities,' and that she enjoys eating fruit gums – like me. ☺

Summary

If you are feeling slightly overwhelmed that there is so much to think about before you even get started, take a deep breath and relax ... Although in an ideal world we would hope to get everything right from the outset, marketing, as with any other skill you may wish to acquire, is something that develops over time. Most things can be adapted as you go along. Indeed, constantly revising and improving your plans and strategies is recommended.

> **Coaching Tip:**
>
> When you are feeling stuck, bored, frustrated or overwhelmed by a particular problem – hopefully not with this complete chapter☺ – instead of asking yourself questions such as:
>
> - Why am I feeling like this?

- Why can't I do this?
- What's wrong with me?
- Why is everything so difficult?

Ask yourself these questions instead:

- What do I want?
- How can I overcome this problem?
- What do I want to be feeling and thinking?
- How can I achieve my result in an easier way?
- How can I change the way I feel right now?

This is because 'why' questions will just tell you where you are now. The second set of questions, however, will tell you how to move forward from this point. So if, for example, you have had a lifelong struggle with getting to grips with the Internet and social media platforms and usually think things like:

- Why does this have to be so hard?
- Why didn't I take a course or get someone else to do it?

try substituting them for these questions:

- What skills am I lacking?
- How can I improve my skills?
- Do I know anyone or is there a book that can help me improve my Internet and surfing skills?

Key Points

- Remain self-disciplined and persevere.
- Structure your day and set aside time to market and move your business forward on a daily basis.
- Address your negative views concerning marketing.
- Understand why some books sell and some don't.
- Develop a publicist's mindset.
- Believe in your book in order to sell with confidence.

- Marketing is not about pushing your book at everyone you meet.
- Plan and test the different marketing methods to see what suits you and your book.

Next Steps

- Develop your marketer's mindset using the PIP formula.
- Understand your market.
- Choose a great title.
- Ensure your cover reflects the content and will attract sales.
- Price your book competitively.
- Compile a compelling blurb.
- Write an author biography of yourself in 150 words or less, if you haven't already done so.
- Seek out people who will benefit from the information your book provides.
- Try to secure some endorsements.

Chapter Two – Using Social Media to Market Your Book

Words, when well chosen, have so great a force in them, that a description often gives us more lively ideas than the sight of things themselves.

Joseph Addison

Introduction

The options in social media are vast and trying to become competent in all areas would be more than a full-time job. It is far better to pick one or two things and do them well, than to divide yourself too thinly. So forget any ideas of being a social media expert and instead focus on finding the platforms that you enjoy and which meet your needs in terms of reaching your target market. Endeavour to learn a little each day and allow your confidence to grow gradually.

Social media is about engagement, interaction and conversation sharing. It is made for people, not robots, so show that you are someone personable, rather than plugging your book like a broken record. A consistent and well-portrayed brand can greatly help your advertising. A brand is relevant whether you are a novelist, a non-fiction writer or businessperson. And as the author, you are the brand and your book is the product.

Some novelists who write in very different genres will write under two names. This is so that their readers can associate a particular name with a certain type of novel and it avoids possible confusion. For example, imagine ordering what you thought was the next thriller from your favourite author titled *The Heart Collector*, only to discover it was a historical romance ... In addition to this, it also avoids alienating readers who would be put off by the fact that a thriller writer also writes romance.

For the non-fiction writer, professional or entrepreneur, your brand represents your values, services, ideas and personality. It can generate loyalty from your readers and make you the envy of your competitors. When people understand your brand, they believe they know what to expect from your writing, which can be a problem if you are not consistent in style or content.

Social networking, although possible in person, is most popular online. It is where groups of individuals using Internet platforms like Facebook come together in order to communicate, make connections and share interests, ideas and information. Social media is a form of interaction between people in which they create, share and exchange ideas, and comment among themselves, in both virtual communities and networks, using mobile and Web-based technologies. To become part of this, you need to have a presence on the Internet, so you can build followers and a community of people interested in what you have to say. The key to this is listening to what others are saying and paying particular attention to the information they are asking for. You can then participate and provide answers to their questions and requests for information. In other words, you can become recognised as an authority on a particular area.

Marketing is an ongoing process and there is no need to wait to start your marketing until after you have written your book. It takes time to build a platform and to build trust.

> *Marketing takes a day to learn. Unfortunately, it takes a lifetime to master.*
>
> Phil Kolter

If you are having problems motivating yourself to market your book and frequently sit at your desk feeling frustrated and negative about marketing, this will actually act as an unconscious anchor, which may be triggered every time you sit down to work in the future. So if you are feeling any of these symptoms, get up and walk away from your desk. The place where you work should be somewhere that your unconscious mind associates with you feeling happy, relaxed and inspired so that you can really enjoy what you are doing.

Coaching Tip:

Russian physiologist and physician Pavlov is widely known for first describing the phenomenon of classical conditioning (anchoring). In the 1890s, Pavlov was investigating the gastric function of dogs. He noticed that the dogs tended to salivate before anything was actually delivered to their mouths and so he set out to investigate further. As a result of carrying out a long series of experiments, he discovered what he called 'conditional reflexes' – i.e., reflex responses, such as salivation – that only occurred conditionally upon specific previous experiences of the animal.

Unconscious anchors are stimuli that call forth states of mind, which are thoughts or emotions, and then corresponding actions. We are constantly affected by and respond to automatic unconscious anchors, but we may not know what they are. This is because the anchors have built up accidentally, over time. In fact, we often think that our mood has nothing to do with us and that it occurs by chance, because these anchors work automatically and we may not be aware of the triggers.

Unconscious anchors can come in many forms. For example, if you are in the habit of squeezing your little finger when stressed and you then repeat this action when you are relaxed, it will stimulate your stress response. In addition to affecting your mood, it can also produce an automatic involuntary reaction. So a certain smell such as candyfloss or bacon may take you back to your childhood. A specific song may remind you of a certain person or holiday.

☺ This proves true in all areas of life. When I sit in the sun in my English country garden with my laptop, where I relax, enjoying the moment, my creative mind becomes inspired. Sometimes it is not always about stopping what I am working on, it is about changing where I am working for a short while. Not always easy in rainy old England!

Always try to leave your marketing on a high point or when you have successfully completed a task. If you stop in the middle of doing something that is causing you frustration, you will be more reluctant to go back to it.

Coaching Tip:

If you are taking a break, enjoy it! But when you are not working, are you really relaxing? Or are you berating yourself for procrastinating? Think about it: if you are watching TV but feeling guilty, telling yourself you should be working, you are procrastinating. But if you are watching TV and don't feel as if you should be doing anything else then you are just relaxing.

Social Media Marketing

Words can change lives. Never before has it been so easy for the general public to share their views and influence others. Social media marketing is the process of gaining website traffic or attention through social media sites. Otherwise known as digital marketing, it enables users to create content that attracts attention and encourages readers to share it with their social networks, thereby potentially reaching more people.

Social media has become a 'platform' that is easily accessible to anyone with Internet access and it is a wonderful tool for building an author/writer platform and leveraging yourself as an expert.

Some social networking sites invite reviews or you might post small samples of your work and ask people what they think. Not only will this provide you with feedback, but it will also get your name recognised. Another benefit of getting people you don't know to write a review is that they will be honest.

Social media is the perfect place from which to build your business, find potential customers and form partnerships, enabling you to exchange ideas, information and opportunities. The key to using social media successfully is in understanding your target audience and building a relationship with them. Visibility is fundamental and you need to exploit all avenues available to you, thereby maximising potential sales opportunities.

It may be tempting to focus solely on promotion, but as with conversations in real life, it should be a two-way interaction. If you talk about yourself and your book all the time, people will eventually become irritated and ignore you. The best way to accelerate your results is to take a balanced approach, showing an interest in others and promoting your work.

In addition to following people who share similar interests and ideas to you, you should also follow the marketing activity of successful authors. This way, you will find that you can learn from them by seeing how they voice their opinions and employ various strategies to market their work.

As there are so many different social media sites it can seem overwhelming at first. Not all of them will be right for you or best for your book – or any other products and services you have to offer. New sites start up all the time. Currently, the five most popular are:

- Facebook: a social networking site intended to connect friends, family and business associates. Best for interacting on a more personal level with contacts, it is the largest of the networking sites and began as a college networking website that expanded to include anyone and everyone.
- Twitter: a very popular instant-messaging system that enables people to send brief text messages of up to 140 characters in length (including spaces and punctuation) to a list of followers.
- YouTube: a video-sharing website on which users can upload and share videos for private or public viewing.
- Pinterest: a virtual pinboard where you can create and share collections of things you like or enjoy. You can also 'follow' and share collections created by other people.
- LinkedIn: a business-oriented rather than personal social networking site. Designed for business professionals, it enables them to share work-related information with other users and keep an online list of professional contacts; which of course they can take offline if the need arises, in the form of emails.

For most people, just focusing on the five sites mentioned here is too time-consuming and overwhelming, so try each of them to see which one or two you prefer, or which works best for your book. Then you can put your efforts into using those often and effectively. The chances are that at first you won't know which will work best, so as a general rule of thumb, we would recommend focusing on the ones you enjoy most.

As explained in Chapter One, when you first start to market your work, you need to have confidence in your product or book. After all, if you don't believe in your book, how can you expect your audience to? To overcome this, we suggest that you take the subject matter of your book and explain concisely or sum up the ten most important things about your topic in about 150 words or less. Even though you may already have been living and dreaming the contents of your book for a considerable period of time, doing this exercise will increase your confidence in both your book and your ability to sell it.

Our book, *My Guide: How to Write a Novel*, could be summed up as follows:

> Told with humour, this comprehensive, step-by-step user guide is for aspiring authors so they can learn to write a novel and for established authors to perfect their work, bring it up to a publishable standard and keep their book in the marketplace.

For the book *My Guide: Manage Fibromyalgia/CFS*, it could be something like this:

> Although there is no cure for fibromyalgia, Rebecca Richmond did just this. In this comprehensive guide, she shares details of the programme and techniques she developed to manage and overcome the symptoms of this debilitating condition.

If we were writing one for *A Song of Fire and Ice* by George R. R. Martin we might say:

> A series of epic fantasy novels set in fictional lands with 1,000 years of history. Chronicling a dynastic war between several families for control of the seven kingdoms against the rising threat of supernatural others who dwell beyond the immense ice wall, this is a story of war, betrayal, political intrigue, sexuality and honour.

For *The Kite Runner* by Khaled Hosseini we might consider saying:

> A powerful and humbling story of corruption, guilt and redemption. The Kite Runner tells the story of Amir. Set against a backdrop of tumultuous events, from the fall of Afghanistan monarchy, the Soviet invasion and the exodus of refugees to Pakistan and the USA to the rise of the Taliban regime.

There is no way you can possibly cover every aspect of a novel in the summary and to do so might spoil it for the reader, so simply give a flavour of what it is about, to tempt the reader. If you are writing a self-help or other non-fiction book, you need to convince your readers the book will contain the information that they need or that will help them.

Once you have your summary, you can then use this as a 'strapline', to sum up and sell your book. A strapline is a succinct, catchy sentence or phrase encapsulating or representing your book, company or product, used for marketing and advertising, by drawing one's attention to a distinctive aspect or feature. Its purpose is to emphasise a phrase that you wish the reader to remember your book by. For example:

- *Necessary Lies* – The best intentions expose the darkest secrets (by Diane Chamberlain)
- *Mindfulness* – A practical guide to finding peace in a frantic world (by Prof Mark Williams and Dr Danny Penman)

Famous examples would include the *Chicken Soup for the Soul* series, featuring a collection of short, inspirational stories and motivational essays solving the problems of the human race. A strapline for this book could be:

> A book filled with positive and uplifting tales that will warm your heart and improve your day.

If you have written a non-fiction self-help book, compile a Q & A of concerns or worries your readers may have on your chosen topic and give reasons why you are the best person to answer them. In other words, clarify why they should buy your book on a certain topic rather than someone else's. Also, consider what makes yours different from what is already on the market. You could even format a list of words readers would use to describe you: friendly, professional, informative, casual, approachable, etc., telling your audience what they can expect from you.

You will then need to come up with some sort of author biography, which is a written piece about yourself. Examples of the type of thing you should write about can be seen as follows:

> Author of *My Guide: Manage Fibromyalgia/CFS*, Rebecca Richmond has enjoyed a highly successful career within global organisations, later going on to become a coach. Having triumphed over adversity and cancer, as a qualified coach and master practitioner of NLP, hypnosis and Time Line Therapy™, she is ideally equipped to help you achieve the success you deserve.

> A qualified proofreader and editor, Claire Pickering knows her subject and has an amazing attention to detail. Having worked in the publishing industry for many years, *My Guide: How to Write a Novel* is her first published work – unless you can count the hundreds of manuscripts she has worked on over the course of ten years, which are now in the general market …

Think about what you know and your background in terms of how it qualifies you to write the book. To give you more ideas on how to connect with your audience, consider some of the following questions:

- What makes you an expert on this topic?
- What are you good at?
- Where did you go to school?
- What do you like or dislike doing?
- What clubs and associations are you a member of?
- When did you first start writing?
- Who are your current and previous employers?

By interacting with people, you can create a loyal connection between yourself, your product and the individual.

Note of Caution – Staying Safe on the Internet

Be aware that you need to protect your privacy and physical safety. It is impossible to be certain who is behind the name and face, and with whom you are engaging. Even if there is a photo, it might not be genuine. Never reveal your home address, telephone number, place of employment or daily routine to strangers online.

> **Coaching Tip:**
>
> Writing a book can be very isolating, but once you start engaging in the various social media platforms you will suddenly find a whole world at your fingertips, so commit to having a conversation with a real person, other than your inner voice, at least once a day!

Each social site has rules. Read them and ensure you follow, apply and understand them if you don't want your page, group, etc. being withdrawn, penalised, suspended or even banned.

As with all things online, read all the terms of service, privacy policies and cookie use prior to signing up for anything.

Choosing a Moniker

When using social media, your posts are generally identified by your username or moniker. For each platform, you will be asked to choose a name to be displayed to your audience publicly. However, as with pseudonyms for author names, with sites like Twitter there is little point hiding behind moniker such as @ibookjunkie47, @annie998 or @scifiguy as people won't be able to identify with you, which defeats the point of your marketing efforts.

If you are using your book to promote your company or business, remember that people will need to engage with you as a writer before they will become interested in what your company has to offer.

Engaging with Your Audience

It is very tempting to become focused on the number of followers you achieve and many people in social media will tell you that that is the key to success. But adopting this philosophy might mean you end up with a very large list of people with absolutely no interest in your writing. The key is in locating people and building a list of people who are genuinely interested in your topic. It is far better to have 500 people who are eagerly awaiting the release of your book and intending to buy it than it is to have 10,000 people who have no interest in it whatsoever.

This means that the emphasis should be on quality, targeted followers who you then engage with on a regular basis. When they have actually read and liked the book, hopefully they will help to spread the message through their own networks, giving you what is called 'organic growth'.

If you do decide to focus on the number of followers rather than targeted followers, of the several thousand you achieve, you will probably find that very few actually get to 'know' you – which is why we encourage you to leverage your fan engagement and network with your followers.

Another thing to bear in mind is that you have no control over how many other people your followers are watching and if they are watching too many people, then the chances are that your posts will be missed. Only by keeping your posts interesting and relevant can you hope to get noticed.

Whilst it might be tempting to comment if someone has just had a baby or posts something about their weekend, it may come across as being false, especially if you frequently give insincere compliments. Instead, be sincere and honest from the outset that you are marketing your work and give help, information and advice on the subject you have written about. Don't just comment for the sake of it, as many hours can be lost answering questions but not really adding value. Perhaps ask yourself the following questions:

- How will this get me where I need to be?
- Will this make a difference to what I am trying to achieve and move me forwards in some way?

How Much Marketing is Enough?

There is no definitive answer to this question. However, you should constantly aim to look for opportunities and new ways to market your book in order to achieve the goals you have set for yourself. Also, be prepared to change and evolve your goals over the course of your career.

Coaching Tip:

When setting goals for yourself, follow these guidelines:

1. Set goals that:

   - Inspire you
   - You feel are achievable

2. Set milestones along the way and reward yourself when you have achieved them.

Setting and achieving goals should be an enjoyable process. If you are not enjoying or achieving your goals, revisit them and ensure you still have a strong enough motivation to achieve them.

The amount of marketing required to achieve sales varies for everyone and will depend on your niche. If you are writing about something specific, like fibromyalgia, then your audience will be smaller. However, if you are writing about something which may affect a wider demographic, like slimming, then you will need to market to a much broader audience. Our book, *My Guide: How to Write a Novel*, has a niche market in that it will only appeal to a certain sector of readers who want to write a novel. For novels, this could include genres such as westerns, sci fi, romance, etc., which may also have a more limited readership.

You also need to take into consideration what goals you want from becoming a published author. For example, you might want to:

- have a book published in your name so you can say you are a published author
- become a thought leader
- make a specific amount of money
- establish yourself as an authority figure and an expert in your field
- appear on Amazon or *The Times* bestseller lists
- share your knowledge with a wider audience

- create a book that can open doors to new opportunities, increased business, speaking engagements and higher fees
- create a legacy to your life's work
- gain the recognition your knowledge, skills and experience deserve
- receive recognition for your creative writing and story-telling abilities
- teach children through storytelling.

Book sales are just for starters. A successful author can make a great deal of money from speaking engagements and of course it opens up other income streams. But perhaps the greatest riches come from knowing that your non-fiction book and the knowledge you have shared in it has helped someone else to improve their life, or that your novel has given many hours of pleasurable reading.

Summary

Whilst we understand the temptation to rush on and begin marketing immediately – after all, that is why you bought this guide – please don't underestimate the importance of planning. It will save you a great deal of time, heartache and frustration later on.

Key Points

- Stay safe on the Internet.
- Read the rules and regulations for each site you decide to build your platform on.
- Engage with your audience.
- Pick one or two platforms rather than focusing on being active on all of them.
- Find the platforms you enjoy and which meet best your needs in terms of reaching your target market.
- Allow people to identify with you as a person.
- Avoid over-promoting your book.
- It takes time to build a platform and to build trust.
- Always leave your marketing on a high point.

Next Steps

- Choose a suitable moniker that people can identify you and your book with and use it consistently on all platforms.
- Decide how much time you can devote each day/week to social networking.
- Consider what platforms you want to appear on and where your potential readers might come from.
- Write a summary of your book and memorise it so that it becomes a rehearsed mission statement.
- Compile a strapline for your book.
- Write down what you would say to convince someone to buy your book in 150 words or 30 seconds.
- Write an author biography in 150 words or less.

Chapter Three – Facebook

It's not enough that we do our best; sometimes we have to do what's required.

Sir Winston Churchill

Introduction

Co-founded by Mark Zukerberg in 2004, Facebook is a social networking service that enables people to connect with friends, co-workers and others who share similar interests or who have common backgrounds. It allows for the sharing of updates, posts and photos, the joining of events and a number of other activities. In other words, it acts as a community.

By 2015 it had over 1.55 billion monthly active users worldwide and 1.01 billion daily active users, with 894 million mobile daily active users on average.[1]

If you are trying to target the 25 to 34 year age bracket, then Facebook is the place to be.[2] One study found that 65 per cent of Facebook users visit the site daily,[3] 'with 54 per cent logging on multiple times a day'.[4] Most users are female, the highest traffic occurring mid-week between 13.00 and 15.00 hours, with highest engagement on Thursdays and Fridays.[5]

Facebook allows you 5,000 characters for each status update. However, this is more than enough as only a small fraction of people will read long pieces of unbroken text and if you adopt this style you risk losing the attention of your audience. Using images and photographs, and focusing on gaining higher levels of interaction, is far more effective than reams of text.

Many use Facebook as a way to stay in touch after finishing university or leaving a workplace, or as a means to share their life publicly.

But increasingly it is becoming used to market and sell. One of the constraints on Facebook is that you are only allowed one Facebook account. Having more than one account is in violation of their terms of use and you can find yourself or your account banned or disabled if you decide to set up more than one.

> People share, read and generally engage more with any type of content when it's surfaced through friends and people they know and trust.
>
> Malorie Lucich, Facebook spokesperson

If you have a business page, fans can message you but you cannot message them until they have messaged you. In other words, you cannot initiate a conversation and it is thereby difficult to solicit 'fans'. For every message received, you can only send two messages back. However, Facebook pages now allow private messages, which helps communication. Business accounts don't show up in search results and neither can they send or receive friend requests or build apps. While they can see public information about other people on Facebook, they cannot interact with those people except as a page.

Confused? In short, a private profile is for personal communication with family and friends. A page is used to feature a business, product or author and a group is where people with similar interests can meet and discuss things.

Setting Up a Facebook Account

We would recommend starting with a free Facebook page or profile, from which you can then set up a fan page for your book. If you go to <http://www.facebook.com>, you will be taken to a screen that asks you to login or sign up for a free account. Click on the 'Sign Up' option, which takes you to a form. Fill out the form, giving your full name, email address, a password, your date of birth and whether you are male or female. Note – by clicking 'Sign Up' you will be acknowledging that you understand and agree to the terms of use, privacy policy and cookie use.

Facebook like to check that you are human and not a computer being used to set up lots of accounts, so you will also have to type in a series of letters and numbers as a security check, otherwise known as a 'captcha'. Click the 'Sign up now!' button when you have completed the form, at which point you will be asked if you want to find friends through your email address. You may decide not to do this because you won't necessarily want to 'friend' everyone on your list. It is far better to friend people individually.

As part of the sign-up process, you will be invited to fill out your educational and work history; however, you can always skip this step until later if you prefer. Once you have filled out the relevant forms, you can complete and authorise the sign-up process by clicking on a link – which they will send you via email – where you will be expected to enter a confirmation code in order to proceed.

Ensure you upload a profile picture in order for people to identify you. This will form part of your online presence and should be consistent with the image you use on all of your platforms. Don't forget to adjust your privacy settings, where you can decide what information will be made available about you and to whom.

Once you have secured twenty-five Facebook fans, you can customise and share your page URL by going to <http://www.facebook.com/username>. When choosing a username, you need to bear in mind that it can only be changed once, should you need to change it at some point in the future.

Once you have created your account, you can add detail to your profile, if you haven't already done so when signing up. Facebook profiles are more detailed than those offered by Twitter, as they allow you to provide videos, photos and longer descriptions. However, Facebook can link back to Twitter, and vice versa. You can also include things like testimonials.

To give you an idea of the type of thing required when creating a profile, on a Facebook page, we have put together the following:

Short Description
NLP Master Coach, Master Practitioner of NLP, Master Practitioner of Time Line Therapy®, Master Practitioner Hypnotherapy, meditation teacher, life coach.

Company Overview
Do you deserve more? With Personal Heights you will be able to find solutions to achieve a balanced life, so you can gain the confidence to achieve your goals and not just dream about them. Unleash your potential and take your life in a different direction – the one you've always wanted ... Make some positive changes in your life and find out what living

really means by taking control, with support from Personal Heights.

Long Description
An accredited coach, meditation teacher, NLP master coach and master practitioner of NLP, Time Line Therapy® and hypnosis, Claire supports people in taking action so they can make positive changes in their lives and reach their own personal heights. Together with Rebecca Richmond, Claire co-developed the award-winning *My Guide* series of self-help, wellness and how-to books designed to improve lives. A published author and qualified proofreader and editor, she takes pride in helping authors achieve their goals, demonstrating expertise in editing, publishing and marketing methods that work. Together, they run self-help book coaching courses.

General Information
90% of people spend more time planning a summer holiday, what to wear or what to buy from the supermarket than they do their own lives. If you are ready to stop procrastinating and start investing time in you then coaching is for you. To move past sticking points you have to take action. No longer do you need to settle for whatever life throws your way. When you do so, you settle for a life of regrets, what-ifs, missed opportunities ... So what is the price to you of staying in your current state? Why settle for second best? Bring your life to life and begin with the end in mind ... Coaching changes lives and it can change your life, too!

Mission
Helping more people to improve their lives and achieve their own personal heights though coaching and a comprehensive range of how-to books.

Awards
Won numerous awards for various titles in the award-winning *My Guide* series of self-help, wellness and how-to books designed to improve lives.

Products
- One-to-one life coaching

- *My Guide* series of self-help, self-improvement and how-to books.
- One-to-one book coaching programme for authors of self-help books

Basic Info
Founded
2015

Location
Enter postcode, town and county.

Contact Info
Phone: Insert your contact number
Email: Insert your email address
Website: <www.personalheights.com>

History by Year (for example):
- Added some new third-party products.
- Set up new group on LinkedIn.
- *My Guide* became award-winning series.
- Published *My Guide: How to Write a Novel*.
- New publisher taken over *My Guide* series
- Currently accepting submissions from experienced professionals, trainers, coaches, therapists and thought leaders

Description
Enjoying helping aspiring and established authors achieve their goal of getting their work published.

When you are creating a page profile you have the option of selecting the type of page you want, such as 'Local Business or Place', 'Company, Organization or Institution', 'Brand or Product', 'Artist, Band or Public Figure', 'Entertainment' or 'Cause or Community', in order to build a closer relationship with your audience. If you are an unknown author you might not be ready to proclaim yourself as a public figure, in which case you would set up a personal account instead.

When deciding what account best suits your needs, don't forget that it is a violation of Facebook's user agreement to use a personal account for anything other than an individual person, so you risk losing access to the account and its entire contents should you fail to convert or if you use a personal account for marketing purposes.

Driving Sales with Facebook

As a result of the sheer volume of posts on this platform, it is harder than ever to get your updates noticed on Facebook. The best way to ensure your updates are noticed and acted upon is to schedule your posts so that they are published when your fans are most likely to be looking at their Facebook newsfeed. This can be awkward when you consider that not all of your account followers will be in the UK and so there may be a time difference. With this in mind, post several times during day and on different days of the week.

Try to devote some time spent posting on Facebook during evenings and at weekends, as this is when people tend to be most active. Consider adding a post about something current or popular and ask a question about it over the course of a weekend. You can also post other people's blogs, articles, etc., to your wall, providing you with additional material for posts when ideas run dry.

Interacting on Facebook can be incredibly time-consuming and it requires a lot of effort. If you are going to use your fan page as a business page, you will need to consider some of the following:

- Who will update the information?
- How often are you going to post?
- Do you want a face behind the brand or are you going to market yourself as a brand only, like some of the bigger companies do?
- What type of information are you going to post?
- What type of audience do you want to attract and what will they be most interested in hearing about?

If you are going to use Facebook as a means to promote your book and business, be upfront about it. Don't 'friend' people as a private individual and then bombard them with constant messages to like your page or visit your website. Facebook wants businesses on the site, which is why they have made the recent changes regarding allowing business accounts, but they are determined to respect the wishes of social users and ensure the platform is not abused.

It can be a little confusing if you are a fiction author as you are not actually a business as such, albeit you are using Facebook for business purposes. However, once you have a Facebook account, you can create what is known as a 'page'. A page is different from a personal timeline in that each account can have a personal timeline and manage multiple 'pages'.

The characteristics of a page are that:

- A page can be managed from either a personal or a business account and lets you interact with other users.
- A fan page is intended to gain followers and enable you to communicate with people.
- A business account has limited functions in that it is primarily used for managing pages and advertising campaigns, which are not visible.
- Business pages are not found in search results.
- Owners of business pages are not assigned a personal profile to complete.

This means you should create a page from your business page, to enable you to connect with people easier.

Timelines

Timelines can tell the whole story or history of a person or company and it is now a mandatory feature of all accounts. Personal timelines are for non-commercial use by individuals, whereas Facebook pages offer tools for connecting people to a topic they are interested in. Facebook pages use the same login information from your timeline, as they form part of the same account you registered with in the beginning.

Timelines enable you to keep a chronological history of all the things you have done on Facebook, telling your 'story'. It is now easier than ever to go back in time monthly and yearly using the timeline feature on the right-hand side. In this area, you can record notable dates, such as:

- when you moved
- when you started business
- when your book was released

- qualifications you have achieved
- when you started a new job, etc.
- details of marketing strategies you have introduced and when.

In other words, you can backdate your business history.

This can be useful if you have released a product or accomplished something of interest. You can even add things from before you became a member. These posts go out to all of your fans and while they can be backdated, don't post too many milestones at once as people will get fed up.

The benefit of the timeline is that it is integrated with apps. These are created by third parties, adding more features and functionality to your Facebook experience.

With timeline, a banner or cover image stretches across the top of the profile. When designing your banner, leave space for a photo or your profile picture to be superimposed over the top of the bottom left corner. To see an example, visit our page at:

<https://www.facebook.com/personalheights>

It is the first thing people will see and so should be chosen wisely.

Your cover image cannot contain calls to action, such as 'buy here', and neither can you encourage people to look at your page or buy your product from this space. In other words, you should not include purchase price, contact information, etc.

Every time you change your cover image it will post onto your wall and thereby go into the newsfeed of your fans, so it is a good idea to keep it updated. The cover image should be a representation of you, your service or your brand only. The image in this space should be 851 x 315 pixels down, with a minimum of 399 pixels wide by 150 pixels tall, but you will need to experiment to see what works best for you. Pixels are dots used to display an image and the number of pixels used to create an image is often referred to as the 'resolution'. Pixels are close together, so that they appear connected, and they display an image as a whole.

> *It is a pretty recognizable brand name. Originally it was "Jerry's Guide to the World Wide Web" but we settled on "Yahoo".*
>
> *Jerry Yang*

Your profile picture should be a small headshot of yourself or your business logo. However, a face behind the brand is thought to achieve better results. The general advice is to start with a picture of yourself until you are big enough that you are a recognised brand that people can identify with, such as CocaCola, Monster Energy, Weetabix, etc. This is where a writer differs from a business, in that it is always going to be about you, because you are the brand, so it may well be worthwhile investing in a nice headshot.

- ☺ We suggest you don't put up a picture of yourself wearing curlers and a facemask, unless of course that fits in with the brand you wish to create. Black-and-white photographs can be very effective.

When people are searching for pages, the profile picture is one of the first things they will see and in effect, it enables people to recognise you. If you don't wish to go to the expense of having a headshot done at this stage, a friend with a decent camera or one who is proficient in using their camera phone may oblige. If you already have a profile picture of yourself on the back of your book/novel, you can of course use this one, which will help people to recognise you when they go to the store to buy it or view it on the Internet.

The size allowance for the profile picture is currently 180 x 180 pixels and will sit at 23 pixels from left and 211 pixels from top of page, showing up as 160 x 160 pixels. You can use any of the photos you have uploaded to Facebook as your profile picture; however, rectangular images will be cropped to form a square. You could also add a seasonal touch to it, such as a Father Christmas hat, an Easter feel, etc., as appropriate. Square images of a brand's logo are also recommended in this space.

Apps

Business pages enable people to view a photo gallery, posts from friends, new likes, new friends you have added, etc. (As an administrator, you will also be able to view notifications and messages, in addition to insights/reach.) These can all be seen at the top of your page and are known as apps. You can show a maximum number of twelve apps, the first four being the most important and the most visible, with the others featuring as drop-downs.

Apps are your opportunity to be your most creative as you can't in the cover image or the profile picture, so they should be visually impressive. Consider including a picture of you holding a copy of your own book, as hopefully your cover image will give an insight as to what the book is about and enable potential readers to recognise it.

The apps are displayed in rows of four. The first four will be the most visible and so your best four apps should be placed here. The photo app is always located in the first position on the first row and your most recent photograph will be displayed first. In other words, make the first four apps that are permanently displayed what is key to your business. You can also use the apps to display calls to action, testimonials or special offers.

One of the most effective Facebook apps for authors and writers is The Author Marketing App. This app enables users to enter details of published titles on Amazon with a link to buy the book. You can also add an author profile, join an email mailing list and provide details of any signings you are attending.

All you need to do is enter the ISBN number of published titles on <http://www.amazon.com>. The only real restriction if you are based in the UK is that because it links to <http://www.amazon.com> and not <http://www.amazon.co.uk>, the price listed is in dollars and not pounds sterling. Under the Author Profile, you can add details such as an author bio, genre, publisher, website and email address. Once you have a fan page, to activate this feature go to http://apps.facebook.com/authorapp/ and a page will be displayed enabling you to get started – it really is that simple!

App custom graphics are 111 pixels by 74 pixels and can be changed by clicking the down arrow on the right-hand side to show all apps. By moving the mouse over the app, you can click the pencil icon to activate the drop-down menu, from where you can edit settings to change the title of the custom tab or add custom graphics.

Don't forget to check the privacy and app settings attached to your Facebook account, if you don't want all your followers to see what you are doing or if you don't want the app builder posting on your behalf.

About Section

In the 'About' section, only the first approximately 160 characters of text are visible, so these first few characters are the most important and should be used to good effect. Use this space to describe what you, your book or your company is about, so that potential readers and new followers can decide whether or not to look any further. In other words, stuff this space with keywords and website links – actively show people what it is that you do. Once they click on the 'About' link, the full services that you offer or details of the books you have written will be listed.

Admin Panels

A feature of the timeline is the admin panel, which appears at the top of the page. Here, you can view statistics on how your page is performing. The admin panel can be hidden from view by clicking 'hide' on the right-hand side of your screen. Functions include:

- viewing page notifications
- inviting friends
- viewing new likes
- current activity – details such as the number of people who have liked your page, seen or clicked on a post, etc.

Reach refers to the number of people who have seen your posts in the first twenty-eight days after a post's publication. This information can be seen in graph format, which allows you to analyse what you are doing right and where you can improve.

As part of the service you will receive an email referred to as the Weekly Facebook Page Update digest, which includes the following categories:

- number of fans added in the last seven days
- total number of fans overall
- number of wall posts
- comments and likes for the last seven days and the previous week
- number of page visits for the last seven days and the previous week.

Check your weekly analytics to assess your efforts and aim for an increase in growth each week.

Engage With Your Audience

Unless you are a well-known author such as J. K. Rowling, you cannot build a community around your book, as no one will be interested. However, if you have written a non-fiction book it is possible to focus the community around a cause or an interest that ties in with your topic. If you focus on building relationships, providing quality information and write great books, you will find that people will be keener to promote you to their own networks and newsfeeds.

Other people can post links on your wall; however, you can set approval so that only certain people can post. You also have the option to open and moderate posts. It is easy to change and edit any posts by using the little pencil icon on the top right of all posts. This feature allows you to delete, hide, notify the post as spam, etc. Both fans and non-fans can send messages to pages, but if you feel it is spam, you can disable the posting and even block or report the user. Remember, you have full control.

There are three ways you can access comments left by your fans:

1. From the drop-down menu beneath the apps area, you can select 'Recent Posts by Others' to view people who have posted directly on your timeline or tagged you in a post.
2. In the box labelled 'Recent Posts' next to the apps area on the right-hand side you can click 'See All' to view posts by people.
3. In the 'Admin' section in the notifications area at the top of your page you can see comments from anyone who has replied to a post, like, etc. By clicking on the notification you will then be taken to the relevant post.

Posts stay live at the top of the activity feed for one week. You can update the content of these announcements to keep them current and refresh them or you can write new posts. You can pin posts to the top of your newsfeed by clicking the pencil icon at the top right of the post. Any post can be starred so that it stands out and these can be reduced in size at a later date; you can also change dates.

Ways to Engage

For authors both fiction and non-fiction there are lots of ways to engage with people, including the following:

- Ask people their opinion about a particular subject within your topic.
- Identify someone who did X, Y or Z best.

- Engage with your audience by asking questions and making provocative comments, encouraging a response.
- Make a prediction.
- Try using techniques like question or quote of the week.
- Ask for help.
- Invite comments and thoughts on a topic.
- Share what you are currently doing, like a progress report.
- Post a 'Message me today ...' remark.
- Post a picture and invite comments.
- Post a 'Send me your thoughts about (your topic) ...' remark.
- Post a 'Come and talk to me about (your topic) today ...' comment.
- Be human – nobody feels comfortable with someone who they perceive as perfect and make sure you appear personable. People want to know that there is someone real behind the façade, with real feelings and emotions.
- Don't always be a 'yes' person. Consider arguing with someone over a point you disagree with, but be tactful, unless part of your marketing strategy is to be controversial.
- Share public events, festivals, book signings, etc., and update this often.
- Ask yourself hard-hitting questions others don't dare ask but are dying to know.
- If you have written a self-help book, you can invite questions on the topic and give free helpful advice.
- Invite people to read your first chapter and comment.
- Keep a notebook and pen handy for when ideas come into your mind.

Creating a Fan Page

A Facebook fan page is essentially the same as a Facebook profile except that it is business centric. This is where members can become your fans and stay current with everything you are doing. They can also write on your wall, learn about any special promotions you are running and talk to other members.

On Facebook you are limited to 5,000 friends, but on fan pages there is no limit. Facebook pages can be easily found with a search engine as they are visible to the public by default. You can also add applications to further engage your audience.

Celebrities are just that because of the extensive following or the number of fans they have. To achieve celebrity status on Facebook, you need to have 5,000 followers on Facebook or 10,000 'likes' on fan pages. If you are prepared to put in the vast amount of time required to build such an extensive fan base, you potentially have the opportunity to become a minor celebrity in your own right.

Top Tips for Building an Effective Page

- Stay on topic and keep updating your page to give fans a reason to come back.
- Post relevant and interesting content on a regular basis.
- Brand yourself an authority with a personality – in other words, ensure you showcase your expertise and at the same time show your personality.
- Make use of other social media platforms. For example, if you have a following on Twitter, then invite them to join you on Facebook.
- Pull in content from YouTube, etc., to keep your page fresh.
- Leverage your email list – in other words, offer people on your list an incentive to become a fan.
- Interact with fans.

Things to Avoid

- Don't post promotional messages or links to your blog on personal Facebook walls.
- Don't overly self-promote – people won't thank you for it. Repeated messages such as 'buy my book' will only serve to annoy. Instead, try getting people to read a sample of your book or post a question with a link to discover the answer to something.
- Just because someone likes your page, it doesn't mean they will be seeing your posts. If they are not interested in your posts, they can choose to unlike your page so

the posts are no longer visible on their wall. Or they can simply hide the posts on your wall so they don't have to see them. Be warned, if you overly promote, this is exactly what people will do if you get on their nerves.

- Follow the 80:20 rule (Pareto Principle): 80 per cent of your messages should be interesting, entertaining or helpful; just 20 per cent should be promotional.

Facebook Groups

Groups can be started by anyone on any topic of interest. They serve as a gathering place for members to discuss topics and share thoughts or opinions. The group purpose should always come before your desire to self-promote. It should encourage interaction between members.

A Facebook group is unlikely to get many fans if it is simply based on your book. A far better idea is to start a group based around a topic that will be of interest to your prospective readers. For example, if you are a wedding planner and have written a book on how to plan the perfect wedding, you could start a Facebook group for dealing with the stress of getting married, writing a great wedding speech or losing weight for your big day. Groups like these are far more likely to be of interest to the people involved in arranging the wedding than just planning a perfect wedding, as they deal with a specific topic or problem. Then, when you give helpful tips, advice and support and genuinely engage with them, they may wish to buy your book.

If you have written a fiction book, you can create a group around things like:

- Great holiday reads – a group for women looking for some light-hearted literature to read on the beach.

- Books you would want your children to read – where parents can suggest books that other parents can use to try to tempt their child into the world of literature, etc.

- Books with a plot line that has a twist in the tale and will get readers thinking – this type of group would be of interest to people who are tired of reading novels where they can guess the ending after the second chapter.

- Thriller lovers, but without the gore and explicit scenes that go too far – where followers could recommend a book that is suitable for the more squeamish among us.

Obviously, the group you create should be based around the genre that you have written for. While people will be recommending books that haven't been written by you, the people joining the group would be interested in your type of book and it would give you the opportunity to tell them about your book and engage with them.

To avoid businesses spamming groups, people and organisations who have Facebook pages are not allowed to post direct to them, though you can share page posts, which are basically posts you paste on your page. The general rule is to avoid spamming altogether.

Word of Caution

If you decide to join a group and bombard them with commercial messages, you will get reported for spamming and your profile or page may be shut down. What you should focus on is building yourself up as an authority figure and someone to follow. Likewise, don't only post content that is on your blog and try to drive traffic to it, as people will think you are spamming. Make sure you really understand how groups work before you set up your own.

Remember to mix content from your own blog with other interesting information from the Net. You can find content by looking at sites like AllTop.com or Technorati, which search for blogs and aggregate popular content on the Net. Be careful when posting shortened links on Facebook, as people will be unsure where they will ultimately lead and so may be reluctant to click on them, for fear of phishing, where people attempt to acquire personal information with the intent of using it fraudulently.

Add a Video

Consider making a Facebook video of up to three minutes. For example: Hi, I'm XXX of XXX I have written XXX My book is about XXX.

The best videos are where you are giving useful information, not just promoting your book or services. Have a look at the ones we have created on YouTube (note the shortened URLs; more about this later):

- Ebook Pricing Structure: <http://goo.gl/MWlSw>

- Book Coaching: <http://goo.gl/t7vKM>
- My Guide: How to Write a Novel: <http://goo.gl/iIoPv>

Paid Facebook Advertisements

If you have a very specific market, you could consider running paid advertising, which allows you to target specific groups, i.e. women aged between 24 and 35 who live in a certain area and have tapestry in their profile.

Ensure your users receive what the advert promises once they click through, and keep it social and interesting. Your adverts should be conversational and, if possible, link them to an internal Facebook page as this will break down your viewers' defences and they will be much more open to you.

Create multiple versions of your ads with different images and text. This way you can check which combinations are most effective.

- In the title include your business or page name, a question or key information.
- In the main body of the ad, provide a clear call to action and highlight the benefits.
- Use a simple, eye-catching image that is related to your advert.
- Target different audiences to determine which groups are most responsive to your adverts.
- Check your campaign performance often. Get basic data about your ads, such as the number of clicks.
- Decide if you want to pay on a cost-per-click (CPC) or cost-per-impression (CPM) basis. CPC advertising, also known as pay-per-click (PPC) is where an advertiser pays when an advert or sponsored story if someone clicks on it; although it doesn't guarantee the individual will stay on your site or indeed buy anything. Advertisers bid on keyword phrases relevant to their target market. CPM advertising, on the other hand, is where you pay when people see your advert (per 1,000 impressions).

- Set a daily budget that will allow you to reach your target audience effectively by setting the maximum amount you want to pay each day – once you hit your daily budget your ad will no longer show.
- Bid prices fluctuate often. Set a bid within or above the suggested range, and check your Ads Manager often to update it when the suggested range changes.
- Beware of using bad grammar, dodgy punctuation and poor spelling – hold on to your reputation.
- Don't try to trick people by offering them one thing and delivering another. Remember: if you are paying per click and your ad is misleading, you will pay every time someone clicks on it, regardless of whether or not they actually buy anything or stay on your site.

Facebook has made a lot of changes since it went public in May 2012 that are designed to add revenue. One of their newest features enables you to promote your posts for a nominal fee. Once your credit/bank card has been charged, the post will go to the top of your friends' newsfeeds several times over a period of a few days. The idea behind this is that more of your friends or followers will see it.

Geotargeting for Advertisers

Users disclose all sorts of personal information on their profile, such as age, gender, language, location, work history, etc. Using this information, as a Facebook page administrator you have the ability to deliver content that is only relevant to specific fans. By targeting specific fans and choosing your audience by language or location, you can customise your content to generate the most engagement for the subset of fans who are being targeted, making the post visible only to them. Third-party applications such as HootSuite enable you to manage multiple client accounts in order to make content relevant. This is a free app; however, paid apps are also available.

Summary

Using Facebook can be an effective way of building up followers and a fan base. But it can also be incredibly time-consuming and if you become involved in continually reading and posting about things other than your topic, you can easily become side-tracked. Never abuse Facebook and always respect the fact that people are using this platform to engage and connect with people. They do not want to be bombarded with sales messages.

Key Points

- Only use images that you own.
- Consider what type of page best meets your needs.
- Stay on topic.
- Follow the Pareto Principle.
- Avoid spending so much time on ineffective social media platforms that you lose sight of your goal.
- Build your community.
- Create a free Facebook page.
- Post content on a regular basis.
- Don't spam and overly promote.
- Choose your photo wisely.
- Use a memorable password.
- Choose a banner photo or image that will look good stretched across the page.
- Don't always be a 'yes' person. Consider arguing with someone over a point you disagree with.

Next Steps

- Set up a fan page or a business page.
- Start following people.
- Start engaging with your audience.
- Consider appropriate milestones and write a list.
- Look at some friends' profiles.
- Look at the profiles of authors or influential leaders in your market.
- Check out the pages of some world-class brands.
- Set up your own profile.
- Design a cover/banner image.
- Start a notebook of ideas you can post about.

- Write a good 'About' section.
- Join some groups.
- Consider what apps you want to have.
- Source some testimonials.
- Link your Facebook account with your other platforms.
- Consider starting a group.

Footnotes

1. See <http://newsroom.fb.com/company-info/> [accessed 23.12.15]
2. See <https://zephoria.com/top-15-valuable-facebook-statistics/> [accessed 23.12.15]
3. See <http://expandedramblings.com/index.php/by-the-numbers-17-amazing-facebook-stats/> [accessed 23.12.15]
4. See <http://www.adweek.com/socialtimes/infographic-gwi-visit-frequency/620122> [accessed 23.12.15]
5. See <https://zephoria.com/top-15-valuable-facebook-statistics/> [accessed 23.12.15]

Chapter Four – Twitter

Handle them carefully, for words have more power than atom bombs.

Pearl Strachan

Introduction

Started in 2006 by Jack Dorsey, Twitter experienced rapid growth in 2008/9 and has over 320[1] million active users tweeting 500 million tweets a day.[2] A public company as of November 2013, most account holders using this platform are from outside the US. It is used by large corporations, celebrities, politicians, TV and radio networks, in addition to the general public. The biggest age demographic on Twitter is the 18 to 29 year age bracket,[3] and according to statistics, 36 per cent of Twitter users check in daily.[4] Twitter allows you to keep people interested in your work and up to date with what you are doing. The site is designed to enable people to share short messages or 'updates' with others.

Although updates show up automatically, if someone is following large numbers of people your tweets can be missed. Therefore, it is important that your tweets are well written in order to increase the chances of them being read.

If someone is following your account, your tweets will appear on their home pages. The biggest constraint is that you only get a maximum of 140 characters (not words) per tweet, so your message needs to be succinct. Whilst this seems very brief, people are more likely to read short messages, which is one reason Twitter is so popular. The optimum tweets are around 100 to 120 characters, as this encourages retweets, in that there is space for your Twitter ID and a few characters of additional text for your retweeters to add something new.

As Cicero stated:

When you wish to instruct, be brief; that men's minds take in quickly what you say, learn its lesson, and retain it faithfully. Every word that is unnecessary only pours over the side of a brimming mind.

> ☺ And as Beatrix Potter once said: The shorter and the plainer the better.

> **Coaching Tip:**
>
> Often we put things off, telling ourselves we don't know how to do them or that we don't have the time. In reality, it is more likely that there is an unconscious reason.
>
> Find yourself somewhere relaxing to sit and allow your unconscious mind to deliver the answer as to why you are avoiding tasks or procrastinating. Often, the answer pops into your head – just like magic. Try it ... you'll be amazed.

You need to be able to reach your fans in an engaging way and you can use Twitter to build up excitement by talking about a launch, but don't overdo it. By tweeting about and including a link to your site you can drive traffic to it. Twitter also makes it easy to keep in touch with business contacts either by private or public messages. It is important to contribute to conversations, rather than just follow people and/or view what they are doing. Get people to interact with you by asking questions of your followers, such as:

- What is your biggest challenge relating to the topic of your book?
- What have you read and loved recently?

To be effective on Twitter you need to focus on a theme or topic that is relevant to your book. For example, women's issues, computer technology, stress, fitness, writing, authors, literary circles, romance, sci fi, etc. Include your chosen theme in your bio to attract and build an audience who shares your interest. You should also stay on topic if you are to keep your followers and attract new ones.

Your messages can also contain links to your other platforms, such as your website, Facebook profile, Facebook fan page, YouTube videos, LinkedIn profile, etc., and also links to articles. Your tweet must include a headline and should entice them to read the article. The purpose of a tweet is to get people either to click a link, engage with you, retweet your posts or enjoy your tweets so that they come back for more.

Be creative with your word choice and make your Tweets stand out like a headline in a newspaper article. Ambiguity can also encourage people to click a link to find out more. However, you need to be mindful not to mislead your readers by getting them to click a link under false pretences and then delivering something completely different to what the title or headline infers.

The term 'Twitter 'storm', is used to describe a story that originates on Twitter and generates a significant amount of attention across a broad audience. For instance, if someone spots something on Twitter, they may decide to retweet it. Their fans may subsequently retweet it to their own fans, until eventually it reaches people with large followings, at which point it can't be stopped. By this stage, the originator of the content may not be included in the tweet and messages can become confused or modified. Remember, if you post an ill-judged remark on a trending topic, you may find yourself in trouble, even if unintentional.

> *Life isn't about waiting for the storm to pass ... It's about learning to dance in the rain.*
>
> *Vivian Greene*

Setting Up Your Account

This process is simple:

- Visit Twitter's home page at <http://www.http://twitter.com>.
- Where it says 'New to Twitter? Sign up', enter your full name, email and password then click 'Sign up for Twitter'.
- You will then be prompted to enter your first, last and username (brand name) that you want to become known as, in addition to supplying a password. For example: personalheights, which will become @personalheights, otherwise known as a Twitter handle. You may be advised that the name you require has already been taken, in which case you need to modify or change the name, before clicking 'Create my account' in the yellow bar at the bottom of the screen.

You can then:

- Browse celebrities, etc., who you want to follow.
- Add contacts you already have by searching your in-box for contacts already on Twitter.
- Search for other accounts you want to follow.

Upload a square picture as your avatar or a picture of yourself, your book cover or your logo. An avatar is a personalised graphical representation of the user. In other words, it is simply a different way to depict the self. If you have several social media accounts on different platforms, using the same image will allow people to recognise you and follow you on more than one platform. Avatars appear alongside your posts, easily identifying you as the author and personalising your contributions.

Twitter Profile

Twitter gives users or brands the opportunity to showcase their products through their profile. They are basically enhanced profile pages, based more on the style of Facebook:

- Log into your Twitter account.
- Go to 'Settings' (which looks like a wheel cog on the top right of your screen).
- Scroll down to 'Design' on the left-hand side of your screen.
- Scroll down to the section labelled 'Customize your own' on the right-hand side.
- Select 'Change header'.
- You'll be prompted to choose an image from your hard drive, with a maximum file size of 2MB. If it is too big, Twitter will shrink it to fit, which may distort it.
- Once you select an image it will upload.

Bios

Bios are particularly important in that they tell people what you are about or what you are interested in, so that people can decide whether or not to follow you and ascertain if you have compatible interests. If you don't complete your bio it may deter people from following you, resulting in fewer followers. Completing your bio shows your audience that you have made an effort. After all, how can someone decide to follow you if they don't know who you are or what topic you might tweet about?

You can also include hashtags (#) in your bio (see later for more information on hashtags – a Twitter keyword search tool). For example, for Personal Heights Coaching (@personalheights), our bio is as follows:

> #coach, #mastercoach, #meditation, #stress, #MasterPractitioner #NLP, #TimeLineTherapy, #SelfDevelopment, #Hypnosis, #SelfEsteem, #BookCoaching, #MyGuide

Twitter Header

This is a long, horizontal image or header resembling Facebook's cover profile. It is advisable to use a dark-coloured background because the bio displays in a light-coloured font. Keep it simple, so that the bio text shows up easily on the bottom half of the image. Don't forget that header images will look different when displayed on a mobile, for example. Your avatar will then be placed in the centre of this image, so you need to ensure the bio text and the avatar isn't obscuring something important on the header image. The recommended dimensions are 1500 x 500 pixels, with a maximum file size of 5MB. Twitter profile photo dimensions are 400 x 400 pixels.

Twitter Background

A background photo can be uploaded in addition to your profile header and avatar. A popular idea is to use an excerpt from your book or a copy of your book cover, which you can 'tile', whereby the image is repeated, so that it appears like wallpaper as a background to your profile and tweets.

You can change your background by going to the 'Design' tab under 'Settings'. From here, you can then select a default background or upload one of your own, like we have done on @personalheights, where we have used an image of the front cover of one of our books, *My Guide: How to Write a Novel.*

Some Basic Commands

Placing the @ symbol before a username shows that you are directly addressing that person, but the tweet is still public in that the person mentioned, yourself and anyone who happens to follow both accounts can see the tweet, but your followers won't be able to, unless they follow both of you. If you want all of your followers to see your tweet in their own stream, you need to start the tweet with a character and not @username. For example, consider the following tweet:

> @personalheights is offering #BookCoaching for #authors & #writers wishing to become part of #MyGuide series of #SelfHelp books.

This tweet would be viewable by @personalheights as the intended recipient, you as the originator of the tweet and anyone following both of you (i.e. followers of @personalheights and you).

However, if you were to tweet with a leading character such as a full stop, @personalheights, you as the tweeter and all your followers would see this tweet; however, it would not be visible on everyone else's newsfeed:

> .@personalheights has launched new #bookcoaching service for #authors of #SelfHelp, #wellness and #HowTo books, designed to improve lives..

The same applies with this next tweet:

> See @personalheights if you wish to become part of the #MyGuide series of #SelfHelp, #wellness and #HowTo books.

Direct Messages

To activate this feature, click the arrow button while directly hovering over a user's tweet. Typing DM followed by a username will allow you to send them a direct private message. Another way is to go to 'Messages' in the top menu bar, type a Twitter username, enter a message and click 'Send'.

Direct messaging avoids clogging up your feed when thanking other users for various things that don't add value. It is a means of engaging with someone else without unintentionally creating spam on respective followers' feeds.

Direct messages should be used sparingly as they may take traffic away from you in that they may click on your username and focus on following you or reading more of your content, rather than striking up a conversation. Another thing to bear in mind is that if you want other people to be able to see your replies to another user, you need to add text before the @ symbol, as mentioned earlier.

Hashtags

Hashtags (#) (are actually links) that enable users to categorise tweets by marking keywords or topics in a tweet, in order to help them show more easily in a Twitter search. If someone clicks on a hashtagged word, all other Tweets marked with that keyword will also be displayed. Hashtags are a tool for generating and participating in ongoing conversations. Any Twitter user can join a conversation by using the same hashtag, thereby spreading ideas quickly. Hashtags hyperlink to conversation threads and by typing the hashtag you can see who is tweeting on a certain topic or keyword.

To use hashtags, first type the hashtag followed by a keyword (note: no space is required between the hashtag and the keyword), so people searching can find a topic easily. However, don't add too many hashtags in your tweet, as this will make your post difficult to read and might come across as spam. There are dozens of popular hashtags. For example:

> #amwriting, #askauthor, #AuthorChat, #author(s), #BestRead, #BookGiveaway, #writingfiction, #WritersBlock.

Experiment with hastags, using singular and plural variants or topics of interest around your subject in order to create a variety of hashtags and then test them to see which are the most effective.

Confused? A powerful tool called tagdef at <http://www.tagdef.com> enables you to discover what hashtags really mean. The following may also help:

Typing:

- #OH at the beginning of a tweet means you overheard it. In other words, it is not your idea.
- #FAV followed by a username will favourite that user's last tweet.

- #GET followed by a username will retrieve that user's last few tweets.
- #SO followed by a username means shout out.
- #WM followed by username means Wicked Monday.
- #MM followed by username means Mention Monday.
- #TT followed by username means Tweeple Tuesday.
- #RTT followed by username means Retweet Tuesday.
- #WW followed by a username means Wednesday Writers/Writer Wednesday.
- #TBT means Throwback Thursdays, when people post photos or reminders of the past.
- #SW followed by username means Super Wednesday.
- #FF followed by a username means Friday Friends or Follow Friday.

The latter is incredibly powerful in that the paid subscription website <http://www.SocialBro.com> tracks this particular hashtag in order to find influential followers, so you can 'manage and analyse your Twitter community'.

You can also use a signature hashtag such as:

> #WritingTip with one that would appeal to a target market, such as #WomenInBusiness, or #therapists, #authors, #FemaleAuthors, #MenInWriting, etc.

Identify your keywords and optimum hashtags and use them strategically in your tweets. A signature hashtag can also represent your brand, for example, we might put #PH (personalheights) or #PHC (PersonalHeightsCoaching) or #MG (MyGuide) or #MGBS (MyGuideBookSeries) or #MGS (MyGuideSeries) so people can easily locate our content.

Rather than just put e.g. #FF and a host of Twitter handles, try to be creative and suggest why people should follow them, such as #FF these debut novelists. With this type of tweet, people will often click on the names to find out what the other accounts are all about.

Once you have posted this tweet or general 'shout out', you can then post a general tweet about something you would like retweeted, such as a link to your blog, book, website, etc. You would do this in the hope that when people go into your Twitter handle after seeing your name having appeared in a general shout out, this will be the first tweet they will see. Hopefully, they may retweet or favourite that post to their own followers as a way of thanking you for the additional traffic they might benefit from as a result of your shout out.

A list of everyone who has tweeted on that particular hashtag is also recorded by various publications such as paper.li and scoop.it. Again, this can increase your traffic if subscribers repost the link in your tweet as an article for part of their publication.

Hashtags are limited to one word and do not support spaces. This can be overcome by using a capital letter to denote a new word; for example, #FridayReads. Anybody searching for Friday Reads would then see tweets containing this hashtag. The same applies to hyphenated words, so self-help would become SelfHelp or selfhelp.

While underscores can be used, it should be done sparingly. The common advice is not to overly hashtag a single tweet. The most effective hashtags are those based on a single word, under six characters. Only numbers and letters should be used in keywords. Special characters such as %, £, ! and & won't work, either. Neither can you start a hashtag with a number; although it would be perfectly acceptable to put something like #writing2016.

Twitter has increasingly been used to throw party invitation hashtags, inviting people to attend a Twitter Party for @PersonalHeights, for example, or to meet up to celebrate certain things. These have become known as events and another popular event is #FridayReads. To join the event thread, you would type in, e.g., #personalheights each time you tweet.

The disadvantage of using hashtags is that when people click on them, an entire new set of corresponding hashtag conversations appear, so they may click on someone else's that seems more relevant, rather than yours.

Twitter Abbreviations

Because of the 140-character limit, people often use abbreviations in their tweets. There are thousands of these abbreviations, so it is worth doing some homework and seeing what best fits with your marketing strategy. For example, RT at the start of a tweet means that a post has been retweeted that was originally posted by someone else. Some common ones you might come across, which the text fanatics among you may find familiar, include:

- AB/ABT (About)
- AFAIK (As Far As I Know)
- B4 (Before)
- BFN (Bye For Now)
- BR (Best Regards)
- BTW (By The Way)
- CC (Carbon Copy)
- CHK (Check)
- CX (Correction)
- CT (Cuttweet; partial retweet)
- CUL8R (See You Later)
- DM (Direct Message)
- DYK (Did/Do You Know)
- FB (Facebook)
- HAGN (Have A Good Night)
- HAND (Have A Nice Day)
- HT (Hat Tip/Heard Through; attributing link to another Twitter user)
- HTH (Hope That Helps)
- ICYMI (In Case You Missed It)
- IDK (I Don't Know)
- JK (Just Kidding/Joke)
- KK (Kewl/OK/Got It)
- LI (LinkedIn)
- LMK (Let Me Know)
- MC (Main Character)
- MS (Manuscript; MSS Manuscripts)
- MT (Modified Tweet)
- NF (Non-Fiction)

- OH (Overheard)
- POV (Point Of View)
- PRT (Partial Retweet or Please Retweet)
- QOTD (Quote Of The Day)
- RE (In Reply/Regards To)
- SO (Shout Out)
- TFTF (Thanks For The Follow)
- TFTT (Thanks For The Tweet)
- TMB (Tweet Me Back)
- TT (Trending Topic)
- TY (Thank You)
- WIP (Work In Progress)
- YT (YouTube)
- (YW (You're Welcome)

MEGO comes to mind here ... (My Eyes Glaze Over)

Finding Influential Followers

Initially, it can be difficult to decide what type of accounts to follow and you should try following a mix of people. The best way to ascertain whether or not they are influential is to look at the number of followers a user has. Following these accounts will provide insight into how effective they are at interacting with their followers. For example, whether or not they are talking about things of general interest and the type of information they share, etc. Learn from their techniques to become an influential Twitterer yourself.

Just because someone follows you doesn't mean you have to follow them back. Be selective and take time to look at their profile or bio to see what type of things they are interested in and what they are tweeting about.

Remember, before following someone, try to organise them by putting into a category in your mind, such as friends, family, work, publishing, editing, certain topics of interest, etc. If you can't then maybe they aren't someone you should be following. Various Twitter platforms enable you to do this simply (see later).

The Best Way to Get Followers

The best way to get people to follow you is to think about what you are going to tweet. People want to connect with you on a human level, but they don't want to know what you had for breakfast. To promote a professional and personable image, consider engaging in some of the following:

- Post a link on your other social media sites such as Facebook to your Twitter account in your status profile, urging people to follow you.
- Include your Twitter link in your signature on any emails you send out.
- Tweet a question to provoke a conversation.
- Email your list, if you already have one, to tell them about your Twitter account. For more information on creating lists, see the subheading login/catch pages in the chapter on websites (Chapter Six).
- If you have a blog, write a post about your Twitter account.
- Tweet a funny image using a platform like TwitPic.
- Start following other people. You will find that once you have followed someone, they will be curious about you, check you out and might even follow you back. Each day, follow 500 new accounts from followers of other accounts.
- Target people by searching on a keyword like 'writing', a genre like 'business books' or phrases like 'need help writing'. Use SocialOomph to find people tweeting on your keywords; see later.
- Try to find influential followers. Hopefully some of them will follow you back. By using sites like <http://www.wefollow.com>, where you can add your own interests. For example, ours might be self-improvement, self-help, publishing, self-publishing and wellness. Hopefully, some of them will follow you back.
- Take time to recognise those who continually retweet/repost your content.
- Tweet about people who have lots of followers by including their handle in your tweets, for example, @darrencockle, @benhatch or @personalheights.

- Thank people by giving them a discount on your book or a book gift token from time to time.

Driving Sales with Twitter

You might not know them personally, but many of your followers are likely to be readers, so it makes sense to assume that the more followers you have, the more likely people are to learn about your book/s. However, not everyone will buy the book.

If you had 1,000 followers on Twitter of whom just 1 per cent read books in your genre, then you would have a potential 10 new fans and customers. Increase this to 25,000 followers and you have a potential 250 new fans; 250,000 followers and you would have a potential new readership of 2,500.

> *The biggest mistake we see companies make when they first hit Twitter is to think about it as a channel to push information.*
> Tim O'Reilly and Sarah Milstein

Your followers will only be interested in what you have got to say if you are following the right people and tweeting about relevant content. But it is not as simple as just going out and getting followers, as there are many limitations to Twitter.

> *The only limits are, as always, those of vision.*
> James Broughton

Limitations

- The most obvious is that you only have 140 characters per tweet.
- You can only follow 1,000 people a day on Twitter; leave room to follow others back who follow you first.
- Each account can follow 2,000 users in total, before a limit to additional users you can follow kicks in; otherwise known as a follow limit.
- If you are following more people than are following you, there will come a point when Twitter won't allow you to follow any more people until you find more followers or unfollow some accounts. This ratio is based on your ratio of followers compared to those you are following.

- Regularly following and unfollowing lots of people is discouraged and can result in account suspension.
- Don't duplicate tweets. Always add new content.

Getting Past the Twitter Barrier

Once you are following 2,000 accounts, the number of people you follow cannot exceed your follower total by more than 10 per cent. You then have two options: either make room for more potential leads by unfollowing people who are not following you back or by unfollowing accounts who are not tweeting information of interest to you. Alternatively, can wait until sufficient people follow you back and you hit the 10 per cent mark, but this can be a lengthy process.

While it is relatively easy to follow people, it is more difficult to unfollow people who don't follow you back. However, there are now Twitter apps like JustUnfollow, which enable you to find people who unfollow you or who don't follow you back. An app is an application, program or group of programs designed for end users to improve their overall user experience. Using the app mentioned here, you can also find your fans, find fans of accounts you follow and whitelist non-followers. Whitelisting is the opposite of blacklisting.

The JustUnfollow app enables you to find all your Twitter unfollowers quickly, so you can decide whether or not to continue following them. With JustUnfollow, you can do the following:

- Find users who don't follow you back.
- Find users who follow you but you are not following back.
- Find users who haven't tweeted recently.
- Unfollow users you are currently following.
- Check your relationship with a particular Twitter user.
- View all users you have whitelisted.
- Follow the followers of any other Twitter account.

JustUnfollow allows you to unfollow up to twenty-five accounts a day. However, if you tweet an automated tweet that states something to the effect that you have 'just found all your unfollowers using JustUnfollow', this limit will increase to fifty users a day.

Whilst this service is free, there is also the option to upgrade to a premium service, so that you can unfollow an unlimited amount of accounts, for a minimal fee. With JustUnfollow Premium, you can:

- have unlimited unfollows
- have unlimited follows
- add multiple Twitter accounts
- Whitelist up to 500 users.

Remember to check your non-followers regularly and allow enough time for them to follow you back before unfollowing them. Go to <http://www.justunfollow.com> to sign up for an account. Others that provide a similar service to JustUnfollow include:

- <http://easyunfollow.com>
- <http://www.friendorfollow.com>
- <http://www.gremln.com>
- <http://www.hootsuite.com>
- <http://www.mediafunnel.com>
- <http://www.tweepi.com>
- <http://www.twitterfeed.com>
- <http://www.useqwitter.com>

Please note that there are many sites other that offer a similar service that can be found through search engines. These are just to give an example and have not been endorsed by us.

Guidelines for Tweeting

Most tweets are composed of smart or short remarks, often containing links, and the following advice may help you:

- Don't duplicate tweets.
- Don't tweet constantly, but tweet often. Stay consistent. We recommend tweeting three to five times a day about different subjects.
- Experiment with tweeting at different times of the day, including weekends.

- Only tweet about things that matter, with the occasional non-relevant tweet to let followers know you are human.
- Don't use tweets to have a personal conversation. It will clog up your tweets and get on people's nerves; for example, 'thanks for the follow/RT'.
- No hard selling, otherwise people will begin to regard your tweets as spam and so you will not build up a good reputation. The majority of tweets should be free of advertising altogether.
- Your main goal should be to provide value. Look back at your old tweets and ask yourself: Are you giving value? Would you follow yourself?
- Stay on topic and be selective with your posts.
- Post insightful, amusing, entertaining, interesting and resourceful tweets.
- If you are having a bad day, say so, but perhaps include a positive side that has come from it.
- Eye-catching tweets should only be occasional.
- Careful what you tweet about. This is your reputation at stake and you alone are responsible for the content.

Things to Tweet About

- Ask provocative questions.
- Tweet about new pages you have added to your website.
- Retweet and comment on interesting things from other people.
- Favourite other users' tweets.
- Offer links to free or interesting content.
- Comment on current events/news.
- Tweet about interesting or exciting things you are doing, such as a book signings or radio interviews.
- Write headlines that sound like news by using blunt, direct statements.
- Make lists that deliver information, e.g. five reasons why you should ...

- Consider writing some how-to tweets.
- If you get a good reaction to a tweet, re-post a week later, prefaced with something like: Did you miss this ...?

Consider incorporating Apple's Twitter address (@iBookstore) in your Apple-oriented tweets or addressing them directly. The Apple store is called the iBookstore, not iBooks, and they call ebooks 'books' not ebooks or e-books. They like to see books referred to as 'on' the iBookstore and not 'in'. Their Twitter handle is a person, not a machine, so bear this in mind when writing tweets if you want them to retweet your tweets.

If you have used WordPress to build your website, install a plug-in that will easily allow your visitors to follow you. A plug-in is a software code that enables an application or program to perform something that it couldn't do by itself. For example, without Adobe Flash Player, you wouldn't be able to view multimedia such as BBC News bulletins embedded into web pages.

Establishing a link between your blog and your Twitter account is essential. If there is no link, you will just be an anonymous tweeter. There are several plug-ins to choose from:

- GroupTweet: lets you send tweets to a select group from the same account by several contributors.
- NewsTweet: when you input keywords or keyword phrases, this plug-in will pull newsfeeds or posts in your niche containing this keyword from Twitter and place them in your side bar.
- Qwitter: sign up to email alerts when someone stops following you.
- TweetDeck: allows you to tweet remotely and track followers, direct messages, etc. Supports multiple Twitter accounts and removes the need to visit Twitter constantly.
- TweetSuite: integrates Twitter and WordPress, automatically tweets about new posts and gives you retweet buttons, etc.
- TweetThis: allows users to share your blog posts on Twitter.
- Twitbin: Firefox plug-in that allows you to monitor your Twitter conversations from your side bar, so you can watch them while working on other things.

- TwitPic: allows you to share your photos and videos on Twitter.
- TwitterCounter: places a counter on your blog stating how many followers you have.
- Twitterfeed: automatically posts your blog updates on your Twitter account via the RSS feed.
- TwitterTools: integrates your blog and your Twitter account, allowing you to post tweets easily on your blog and put blog links on your tweets, all from the WordPress control panel.

Websites that help Twitter users include:

- <http://www.Twitaholic.com>: ranks Twitter users by the number of followers and provides statistics on your followers if you sign up.
- <http://www.Twellow.com>: a *Yellow Pages* for Twitter users.
- <http://www.Tweriod.com>: tells you when your followers are online, so you can ascertain the best time to tweet.
- <http://www.Twiends.com>: find users with similar interests.

Paid Advertising on Twitter

Paid advertising enables you to achieve quick results when promoting yourself and your book. You can choose to promote either your tweets or your account. If you choose to promote tweets, Twitter either automatically selects tweets or you can select them yourself manually. The promoted tweets are displayed at the top of relevant search results and can be targeted to user timelines.

If you promote your account, in order to increase your follower count, Twitter will display your account prominently in the 'Who to Follow' section for users who would most likely be interested in your content. Only your account name will show up, so it is vital your account name attracts followers.

There is also a feature through which you can promote trends, whereby users who click on one of these see search results for that topic and they feature prominently next to a user's timeline.

Things to Avoid

As with most things in life, too much of a good thing can be bad:

- Don't automatically follow everyone who follows you.
- Be selective when finding people to follow.
- Don't ignore your fans. Set aside time to engage with them by commenting, retweeting, etc., as following people alone is not enough.
- If other users are just scouting for more followers for their own popularity, you might consider giving them a miss.
- Avoid spending so much time on ineffective social media interactions that you lose sight of your goal.

Things to Do

- Check out who a user is before following them, to see if they are tweeting about things you are interested in or if they might be interested in something you have to offer.
- See if you can determine whether or not they look like a key influencer or if they have thousands of followers, in which case they might be receptive to retweeting some of your tweets to their fans.
- Consider using Hootsuite or TweetDeck to create what is known as Twitter lists, so that you can categorise followers. For example, Colleagues; Fans; Friends; Media; Services, etc. If a follower doesn't fit into one of your list categories, then maybe you shouldn't be following them. Lists will make it far easier for you to keep track of people.
- If you are running a conference, book signing or other event, promote it through Twitter hashtags.
- As with all social media platforms, engage with your audience and let them know that you are human.

Using SocialOomph to Automate Twitter

First created in 2008 by Dewald Pretorius, SocialOomph enables users to set an unlimited number of schedules in advance. This saves time in that you can schedule tweet comments on the time and date that you want it to appear throughout the day, in advance. You will need to upgrade your membership if you wish to do the same with Facebook and LinkedIn. SocialOomph also enables you to attach links and articles to your tweet and you can shorten URLs, which helps with the maximum 140 character tweets.

Once you have a SocialOomph account, you can set it up to receive a digest of tweets that contain specified keywords in the form of a daily email summary, thereby targeting people who post articles or material using specific keywords. In other words, whenever someone posts an article containing one of your keywords, you will receive a daily email of results. From this digest you can then choose to follow people who are tweeting about relevant topics or whose profile seems interesting.

Creating an Extended Profile in SocialOomph

The user profile or bio area in Twitter is limited, enabling you to add a very small amount of text and one URL. With SocialOomph, you can create a detailed profile with lots of text and as many links as you want. The extended profile will automatically show as a link in the Twitter profile area.

How to Schedule Posts in Advance on SocialOomph

Otherwise known as scheduling updates, it is relatively simple to post tweets in advance:

- Go to the black bar at the top of the screen and click on 'posting'.
- Click on 'create new update'.
- Type in your text.
- Shorten URLs using inbuilt feature.
- Select a date and time you want your tweet to appear.
- Select the account you want the tweet to be scheduled to (you can have up to five Twitter accounts linked to your SocialOomph account).
- Click save.

Remember to schedule some tweets at night, to catch traffic from other countries. If you are scheduling tweets to include a link to Amazon to buy your book, bear in mind that people the US may not want to buy a book in pounds sterling and vice versa, so ensure you include links to both Amazon sites – <http://www.amazon.com> and <http://www.amazon.co.uk> – for both your book and your eBook.

You can also set up a welcome DM (direct message). For example, every time someone follows you on Twitter, you could send an automated message to include something like:

- Thank you for choosing to follow Personal Heights Coaching. We hope you enjoy our tweets/Twitter stream and we look forward to chatting to you.
- You could ask them to check out your blog or website and include a link, etc.
- Or invite them to follow you on your Facebook fan page.

To change your auto DM welcome message:

- Login to your account.
- Select 'Following' on the bar at the top of the screen.
- Click 'Follow-Back & Auto-DM'.
- Select 'Configure'.
- Locate your Twitter account in the list of accounts.
- Change your automation settings and welcome message, up to a maximum of 130 characters.
- Separate each DM with a pipe [|] symbol.
- Click the 'Save' button.

An example would look like this:

> {Welcome to Personal Heights. Thank you for following. Having trouble with self-esteem: http://www. personalheights.com/|Welcome to Personal Heights. We are also on Facebook: https://www.facebook.com/ PersonalHeights|Welcome to Personal Heights. View our website: www.personalheights.com|Welcome to Personal Heights. Feel free to view our blog http://www. personalheights.com/blog|Welcome to Personal Heights. Feel free to view our website: www.personalheights. com|Welcome to Personal Heights. Find us on Twitter

@PersonalHeights|Welcome to Personal Heights. Join us on LinkedIn:https://www.linkedin.com/company/personal-heights|Welcome to Personal Heights. Find us on Google+: https://plus.google.com/b/105367335005223886024/+PersonalHeightsHengoed/about}

SocialOomph rotates the automated DM messages for you. Sending a welcome DM increases chance of the follower favouriting or retweeting your tweets. There are many other features on SocialOomph and it is well worth a look at their site. It is an excellent tool for automating the social media process as far as possible, leaving you free to get on with other marketing strategies.

> **Coaching Tip:**
>
> Don't let fear hold you back. Many writers are concerned about the fear of failure, rejection and being judged. If this is an issue for you, consider the following:
>
> Fear of failure – if you actively market your novel or book and it does not become a bestseller or even sell any copies, at least you will have learnt how use the marketing platforms, and hopefully enjoyed the experience.
>
> Fear of rejection – not everyone will like you or your book, but that is just part of life and you will be in the company of some very successful writers. The ability to carry on when things don't work out is the determination of champions. Remember that reading is like so many other things in life in that it is subjective and purely a matter of taste, just like our opinions in this guide!
>
> Fear of being judged – often, writers are anxious about people laughing at their ambitions. People will judge your writing and you, but almost everyone either respects people who are willing to try, and often when they don't respect the efforts of others it is because they know they are too afraid to do so themselves. ☺

Summary

Twitter is a community – joke, offer compliments. Establish a repertoire with your followers. If you are informal, they will see you as a regular person they can relate to.

Be direct with your bio. Tell people who you are and what you do, in addition to providing them with any professional credentials you may have. Include your website URL, as well as details about recent publications and significant events. Make full use of hashtags. Anyone can create them by adding a hashtag in front of a word or phrase with no spaces.

Vary your tweets. On Twitter, if you post something more than once, it will tell you 'oops, you have already said that', and it therefore won't allow you to become repetitive. It is possible to download a Twitter archive by going to 'settings' and clicking 'Request Your Archive'. A file containing all of your tweets will be emailed to you for downloading.

Don't let the restraint of 140 characters put you off. After all, you have already proven that you can write a whole book and Twitter have even hosted at 'twit fic lit fest' as an online storytelling festival, with users even writing a book on Twitter. Authors such as Ian Rankin, Jilly Cooper and Jennifer Egan have all managed it, proving that anything is possible. To view or follow, use the hashtag #twitterfiction to see what it is all about.

Key Points

- Aim to follow someone each day who tweets regularly.
- Retweet other people's articles and activities.
- Embrace Twitter limitations and the 140-character restriction – use it to sharpen your writing skills.
- Engage with your fans by asking questions and giving value.
- Build excitement for any launches or key events around your book or new products relating to your book.
- Keep a log of things you can tweet about for when you run low on material.
- Use links and Twitter apps/plug-ins to their full advantage.
- Take time to acknowledge people who retweet, mention or favourite your tweets.
- Experiment with tweeting at different times of the day and week.
- Don't duplicate tweets.
- Eye-catching tweets should only be occasional.

- Don't automatically follow everyone who follows you.
- Post material three to five times a day. If this really feels like too much, post one quality tweet per day.
- Keep relevant with your tweets; unless you are a celebrity, nobody will be bothered that you are in the supermarket at the deli counter.
- Remember – no hard selling.
- Everything on Twitter represents your brand.
- Keep your reputation intact.
- Don't get addicted!
- Have fun – Twitter is the future!

Next Steps

- Set up a Twitter account.
- Decide on a good Twitter name or moniker (as discussed in the chapter on Facebook).
- Upload a picture or avatar.
- Create a header or cover image.
- Make full use of your background.
- Browse some celebrities and influential followers to see how they are doing it.
- Write a good Twitter bio and be creative with your word choice.
- Start following people.
- Post some tweets, including links and articles/blogs.
- Practise using some of the basic Twitter commands, abbreviations and hashtags, to ensure your tweets are noticed.
- Sign up for a SocialOomph account, schedule some tweets and set up a welcome DM.
- Sign up to JustUnfollow.
- Have a look at what Twitter plug-ins might be useful to you.
- Target people using keywords and hashtags.
- Link your Twitter platform with your other social media accounts.

Footnotes

1. Statistics taken from <https://about.twitter.com/company> [accessed 23.12.15]
2. See <http://www.internetlivestats.com/twitter-statistics/ [accessed 23.12.15]
3. See <http://sproutsocial.com/insights/new-social-media-demographics/> [accessed 23.12.15]
4. See <http://venturebeat.com/2015/01/09/heres-how-many-people-check-facebook-twitter-and-instagram-daily-in-2-graphs/> [accessed 23.12.15]

Chapter Five – Linked in, YouTube and Pinterest

Many of life's failures are people who did not realize how close they were to success when they gave up.

Thomas Edison

Introduction

We have now covered the two main platforms, but there are plenty of others to choose from and we have listed a selection of these in this chapter. We suggest that you try one or two of the ones listed in this next chapter, in addition to Twitter and Facebook.

> **Coaching Tip:**
>
> Your mood can affect your work and vice versa. It is well recognised in the field of psychology that your mood at any given time affects how you perceive the world around you. If you are feeling happy and optimistic about your marketing techniques, you will view events from this perspective. If you are feeling unhappy or anxious, your response to situations will be a reflection of this mood.
>
> So if you are feeling down, anxious or angry, this is probably not the best time to respond to comments or engage with people on a social media platform. Unless of course you are intentionally building your profile as a blunt or grumpy person as part of your marketing strategy – although we don't suggest you become a Victor Meldrew. ☺

On the other hand, if you have just spent all day tweeting or writing about traumatic or horrific events, don't be surprised if at the end of the day your mood is dark.

How to change your mood:

If you have been focusing all day on dark and depressing topics, it is likely to send your mood spiralling in the same direction. So if you are feeling anxious, down or irritable and simply want to change your mood, it really is very simple: spend some time, just five to ten minutes, thinking about pleasant and happy things. Play some upbeat and happy music. Smile, get up and move around or dance. You could even go and sit somewhere else for a while and have a change of scenery.

LinkedIn

A lot of social media sites are designed for fun, but LinkedIn is intended to connect people professionally and allows people to create company profiles as well as personal ones. We are particular fans of LinkedIn and we think it is a great platform to connect with people who may require our services. But LinkedIn is far more than a way to generate business – it is also a great place to engage with other people in our industry, share ideas and network.

If you have written a self-help, non-fiction or how-to book, in order to establish yourself as an expert in your field, we would definitely recommend that you have a presence on LinkedIn. You could even consider starting a group around your chosen topic.

As a fiction author, it is an ideal platform for connecting with people in the publishing industry and other like-minded authors, who will often be willing to share their experiences around all aspects of writing, publishing and book marketing.

Founded in the living room of Reid Hoffman in 2002, LinkedIn was officially launched in 2003. With over 400 million users in over 200 countries and territories, it is the world's largest professional, business-related social networking site for business owners, entrepreneurs and professionals.[1] Using widgets, members can promote their various social networking activities, such as Twitter, Facebook, blogs, etc., on their LinkedIn profile. According to statistics, just 35 per cent of LinkedIn users check in daily, which is worth bearing in mind if you need a higher level of engagement.[2]

LinkedIn gives its members the opportunity to:

- Build a 'Company Page' that allows business owners to promote their products or services, interact with their customers, generate sales leads and connect with potential business partners. This gives them a better way to capitalise on the social power of this platform.
- Search for other professionals and thought leaders.
- Join some groups.
- Give and receive written recommendations.
- Both receive and endorse a connection's credentials at the click of a button.
- Research products and services.
- Link up with other companies, publishers, writers, authors, social media experts, marketing gurus, etc.
- Receive the latest updates and industry news.
- Post questions.
- Search for job opportunities.
- Create a group of their own.

When someone Googles you, your LinkedIn profile will invariably be displayed near the top of the page of search results, which is another advantage of having a LinkedIn account. Your profile is important and should contain keywords, as it may be the first thing people see about you when searching on the Internet.

Creating a LinkedIn Account

It is extremely easy to set up a LinkedIn account. Go to <http://www.uk.linkedin.com>, fill out your name and email address, and enter a memorable password. Once you have clicked 'Join now', you will be required to verify your identity. Finally, you can start building your network, following people and groups, commenting on posts, and searching for potential business partners and job opportunities.

You can also connect with people you already know on LinkedIn, such as past and current colleagues, as well as new people.

First, you will be invited to create a professional profile, where you can provide information such as employment status and country of origin, using various drop-down boxes. This is one of the most important aspects of your account and you should make the most of this opportunity, providing as much detail as you can to promote yourself, your book and your business. Your profile highlights education and past work experience, which makes it similar to a CV or résumé. Details on your profile should be kept professional.

Update your profile regularly, so that it stays current. Also, when you update your profile, those who follow you receive a weekly report of changes you have made to your account, giving you increased visibility.

There is lots of scope to make connections and source information on LinkedIn, and suggestions are flagged up on the right-hand side of your screen on your homepage. For instance, you will be able to determine:

- people you may know
- ads you may be interested in
- what groups or whose account you recently visited
- who has viewed your profile
- who has viewed your updates
- how many connections and new people are in your LinkedIn network
- jobs you may be interested in
- groups you may like
- companies you may want to follow

Driving Sales with LinkedIn

As with other social media sites, it is not simply a case of offering your book for sale and waiting for the orders to come flooding in. It is, however, possible to generate interest in you as an author on LinkedIn, which in turn might lead to book sales. Another way in which LinkedIn can help is by assisting you to connect with publishers, agents and booksellers, who may be able to help you promote your work.

In order to get the most from LinkedIn you need to be active, which means contributing to discussions and posting updates. While you can post company news or news about your latest book and create dialogue, the main way you will achieve book sales via LinkedIn is from recommendations and reviews. By contributing to groups you may also increase your credibility as a writer and professional.

LinkedIn Groups

Join several groups. Locate suitable groups by using the search box on your LinkedIn menu bar, change the drop-down to the left of the search box to 'Groups' and enter your desired keywords to find groups relevant to you. There are two types of group: open groups (where you can view content without joining) and members-only groups (where you have to become a member before you can see or have access to the content).

The more members the group has, the more visible anything you post within these groups will be; the same applies when you actively take part in and join discussions. To begin with, participate in conversation threads that have already been started.

Aim to be one of the first to respond to a discussion within a group and to reply to other responses left, so that you are engaging with your audience. This is because most people only read the first few responses to a thread. Better still, start a group of your own … (see later).

LinkedIn allows you to see what groups your connections are in and your connections can recommend groups you might like to join. Each group has statistics available to view, which enable you to view the group activity, so you can see things like:

- who the top influencers and contributors are each week
- who engages highly
- how many new members have joined each week
- when the group was started
- how many comments have been made each week
- location
- total number of members
- weekly growth rate
- total number of discussions the previous week
- number of jobs posted each week
- amount of promotions posted each week
- when it was created

- type of group
- whether or not there are any subgroups
- group owner
- website details
- similar groups
- how many members are already in your network, belonging to a particular group

These statistics will enable you to ascertain whether or not the group is right for you. To view the statistics, go to the italicised 'i' icon to the right of the group name you have clicked on then click on 'group statistics'. If you have more comments than discussions in a group it is a good indicator of highly engaged members, showing real activity.

Once you are a member, you will be able to determine:

- your level group contribution or activity
- latest group activity and discussions

You will also be able to follow member activity within the group.

Always check out each group's rules on their profile, which can also be found using the 'i' icon, to ensure you don't infringe any of them. For instance, some groups won't allow self-promotion, others won't allow you to post links to other sites, some won't allow certain types of topics or discussions, etc. Some groups require membership to be approved in the first instance, which can take a few days, depending on how well the group is moderated.

You can choose whether you receive daily, weekly or no notifications when something new is posted within the group. When this email or 'digest' starts coming through, you can then join discussions that look interesting and begin making your mark.

As with all social media platforms, it is not enough to join groups – you have to participate in conversations. Remember, by initiating discussions that generate comments, you can also become recognised as a top influencer in the group's sidebar/statistics. Before joining a discussion, we would encourage you to see what others are posting first before jumping in with your own views. This strategy also avoids repetition and embarrassment if someone else has already said the same thing, as it shows you have bothered or taken the time to read what else has been written.

LinkedIn also has a facility whereby 'People You May Know' are flagged up, enabling you to find even more relevant connections. Over time, you may find that your interests, goals and priorities change, in which case you can leave groups with less relevance and try out some new ones, so you can connect with others and build your network more effectively.

LinkedIn Tips

- If you have created your own group, you can send an announcement to your members about your product/s and service/s.
- Become known for being knowledgeable in your field by being the first to respond to questions.
- Sales are targeted, in that you will already be connected to influential, professional people in your niche.
- Join discussions in other groups where you can reach an established membership.
- Answer questions that haven't already been answered, such as concerns, problems and issues, to raise your credibility as an author.
- Be opinionated, interesting and provocative if you are to encourage a response. For example, 'Has XYZ had its day?' Provoke a reaction.
- Be inventive with your profile so you stand out.
- Update your profile regularly, as anyone who is following you will receive an email update giving details of new things you have done or skills you have added.

Things to Avoid When Using LinkedIn

As an author, you need to bear in mind that your writing venture is a business and as such, you need to remember that LinkedIn is for business users. Before embarking on using LinkedIn as a normal social media platform, there are a few things you should know about, in order to avoid running into issues:

- Check your spelling and grammar for accuracy.
- Read each individual group's rules carefully, to avoid violating them.

- Always connect with people you know rather than sending an invitation to connect stating you are a friend, when you aren't.
- If you try to connect with five people who you don't know, LinkedIn will automatically place you on what is known as a blacklist, which is difficult to be removed from. In some cases you can email them and explain the situation, but it is better to avoid the situation in the first place.
- If one of your group managers marks your posts as requiring moderation, this is automatically applied to all your posts in all your groups. To get this lifted you will have to contact each group manager individually (otherwise known as SWAM: Site Wide Automatic Moderation).
- When inviting someone to connect, always write a customised message.
- Always use an image of yourself for your profile, not one of your book cover or logo.
- Consider your branding, as this is the first thing people see. For instance, 'Author of spiritual healing books'.
- Be honest on your personal profile – never lie or embellish the truth.
- Posts need to be targeted, so instead of posting updates to every single group you belong to, post to different groups each day.
- Status updates appear on the newsfeed of all of your connections, so don't post too many at a time.
- Consider misspelling your name on your profile, etc., so that LinkedIn see it is one and the same person. For instance, O'Brien and Obrien/OBrien; also the variants Brian and Bryan. You could even include the typo Brain, because other people might misspell your name when searching for you. This is particularly the case with non- standard names.
- Recommendations are key, preferably from people you have worked with in the past, that can be verified.

LinkedIn Status Updates

This feature enables users to communicate with their network on a frequent basis. It can be found next to your profile picture on your profile page and can be updated as often as you like. However, just like Twitter, they are limited to just 140 characters and can contain links.

Status updates are distributed to your network via a weekly 'Network Update' email and your latest update is always displayed on your profile. Status updates of all your network connections are displayed on your home page. However, you need to bear in mind that not everyone checks their homepages and so may miss your updates. They may also choose to hide or comment on your updates.

The type of things you could include in a status update are:

- a new book release/launch
- videos and images
- useful advice or information
- key work/company activities
- a question
- a news article or blog you have read and found interesting
- a quotation
- announcement about you or your company
- events you are organising or attending
- thoughts, views and opinions
- other people's updates shared to your connections

Things to avoid when making a status update:

- overly promoting
- posting too many updates – this is not Twitter
- making reference to clients, thereby breaching confidentiality
- libel, slander and bias, at risk of stating the obvious
- highlighting inexperience
- sensitive or controversial topics
- posting inconsequential information, such as what you had for tea – remember, this is a platform for professionals.

LinkedIn Company Pages

If you have written a book to promote your business, a LinkedIn company page is useful. Currently, there are few people utilising the LinkedIn company pages to their full extent and many are not consistently updated. Because the stream is not yet crowded, it makes sense to start a company page. Only you can decide if a company page is the best approach for you, but you should share information consistently to your LinkedIn company page and profile.

It allows businesses to:

- tell people about their company news
- explain products, services and events
- engage with followers
- share career opportunities

In order to qualify for a company page, you must own a personal LinkedIn profile, with a true first and last name.

Creating a LinkedIn Company Page

To set up a company page:

- Move your cursor over 'Interests' on the menu along the top of your screen.
- Go to 'Companies'.
- Click 'Add a Company' on the right-hand side of your screen near the top.
- Enter your company name and email address.
- Click 'Continue'.
- Confirm your request through an automatically generated email.
- Start filling in your company information – note that the first 156 characters of text are previewed by Google, so these need to be the most relevant, powerful and keyword rich.

And that's it!

There are lots of great ways to personalise your page, so be sure to take advantage of any product features and services. Don't forget to make the page your own. To give you an idea what to put, we have shown you the type of thing we have done:

Company Description
Personal Heights offers coaching and meditation programmes, specialising in self-esteem, self-development and stress management solutions.

Do you deserve more? With Personal Heights you will be able to find solutions to achieve a balanced life, so you can gain the confidence to achieve your goals and not just dream about them. Unleash your potential and take your life in a different direction - the one you've always wanted ... Make some positive changes in your life and find out what living really means by taking control, with support from Personal Heights solutions.

90% of people spend more time planning a summer holiday, what to wear or what to buy from the supermarket than they do their own lives. If you are ready to stop procrastinating and start investing time in you then coaching is for you. To move past sticking points you have to take action. No longer do you need to settle for whatever life throws your way. When you do so, you settle for a life of regrets, what-ifs, missed opportunities ... So what is the price to you of staying in your current state? Bring your life to life and begin with the end in mind ... Coaching changes lives and it can change your life, too!

Claire Pickering is an accredited coach, meditation teacher, NLP master coach, Time Line Therapy® and hypnosis, who supports people in taking action so they can make positive changes in their lives and reach their own personal heights. Having co-developed the award-winning *My Guide* series of self-help, wellness and how-to books designed to improve lives, as a published author and qualified proofreader and editor, she takes pride in helping authors achieve their goals, demonstrating expertise in editing, publishing and marketing methods that work. She now runs self-help book coaching courses for those wishing to write for the *My Guide* series of self-improvement books, which is currently accepting submissions from experienced professionals, trainers, coaches, therapists and thought leaders, commanding them a better income and gaining them status in their chosen field.

Specialities
Coaching, Meditation, Self-Esteem, Stress Management, Stress Reduction, Personal Development, Self-Development, Beliefs and Values, Goal Setting

- Website
  <http://www.personalheights.com>
- Industry
  Health, wellness and fitness
- Type
  Self-employed
- Company Size
  Myself only
  Founded
  2015

Establishing Your Own LinkedIn Group

Once you have joined a few groups and participated in some discussions, you may decide to set up a group of your own. The advantage of having your own group is that you can:

- Make the rules about what can be discussed and whether or not you are going to allow promotions.
- Create a welcome email for new members that includes details of any services you offer.
- Email all of your group members directly once a week.
- Build yourself as an authority figure in your field.
- Select up to three discussions as 'Manager's Choice' to be displayed at the top of the group's home page.
- Make your group name keyword rich so people can find it easily.

- Become recognised as the owner of the group on the group's profile page.
- Set your group up so that you can moderate comments; we have set ours up so that the first three posts are moderated.
- Gain exposure to your professional profile.
- Easily determine who the group's key influencers are.

Other advantages include:

- From a personal account, you can only participate in answers to group discussions. If you have your own group you can set your own discussions.
- Other members of the group can post questions, so that the emphasis isn't always on you, as the group owner.
- Once you have a few hundred members, you will find the group can run itself with minimal input from you, as the manager.
- As the owner and manager of the group, you can assign other members to be managers or moderators, thereby freeing up your time.

Getting Started

Creating a group is really very simple:

- Move your cursor over 'Interests' on the menu bar at the top of your screen.
- Select 'Groups'.
- Click 'Create a group'.
- Fill out the details of your group, including name, logo, summary, description, website, etc.
- Click 'Create'.

Once you have created your group you can:

- Send announcement emails.
- Invite other connections on LinkedIn to join your group.
- Create a custom welcome message.

- Set out your group's rules.
- Post your first discussion.

Example of group rules for our group Therapists, Coaches and Trainers (TCT):

1. We will be unable to approve any posts which are merely a greeting, introduction or an attempt to promote your book, company, services or increase traffic to your website.
2. Please do not make multiple posts on the same topic.
3. All posts should be related to coaching, training and therapy with the aim of fostering genuine conversations and connections with other established and aspiring coaches, trainers and therapists.
4. Please don't post spam in response to a discussion.
5. Respect for the opinions and thoughts of other members of the group is paramount and must be adhered to at all times.
6. Please ensure that any content posted is copyright to yourself and that you have the right to use it.
7. Any posts containing abusive language or profanities will not be approved and you will find that you are removed from this group.
8. Enjoy your writing!

Make sure you visit the group regularly to manage all discussion submissions, and to moderate and respond to posts and requests to join. Ensure discussions are posted in the correct place, e.g. under 'discussions', 'jobs' or 'promotions'.

Difference Between Endorsements and Recommendations

As a LinkedIn user, you will be able to leave endorsements and recommendations for other like-minded professionals. When you create an account you can list your skills and expertise on your profile. Other users can then click on a particular skill listed in your profile to endorse it, confirming that you are competent in this area.

A recommendation, however, is a written statement from one of your connections. It is where they are able to recognise or commend your skills and they are best written by authority figures who people know and trust.

YouTube

Created in 2005 by three former PayPal employees, YouTube is a video-sharing website on which users can upload, view and share videos. Their early headquarters were situated above a pizzeria and Japanese restaurant in California. The YouTube rage caught on and by the end of 2015, it had over a billion users, amounting to almost a third of those on the Internet. Daily, hundreds of millions of hours of YouTube videos are watched, generating billions of views, with most traffic coming from outside the US.[3]

You can use YouTube to create advertisements to promote a particular product or service using a video. You can also sponsor a video. For example, if you searched for a YouTube video on potty training, you may be presented with a sponsored video from a company selling products for babies and toddlers in the results for your search, along with other videos.

Consider joining the YouTube frenzy by making one video for each day, week or month of the year. If you try to become a regular contributor, ensure to follow through on this commitment. Don't begin by posting daily, then drop off to weekly, then monthly. It is far better to start monthly and then build up to weekly and then daily if you decide you really enjoy the process or are getting the results you want. Videos should be two to five minutes in length. It would be more advantageous to have several videos, each two minutes long, than to have less stretching to several minutes or even quarter of an hour; otherwise, you will lose the attention of your audience.

Creating a YouTube Account

To create an account:

- Click 'Sign In' in the upper right-hand corner of YouTube.
- Follow the steps, depending on whether or not you have a Google account, as Google owns YouTube.
- If you already have a Google account, sign in with your Google account email address and password.
- If you don't have a Google account, you will be asked to create one as part of the sign-up process; this is for

your new Gmail email address only. All you need to do is click 'Create Account' and enter the information required.

- If you don't want your name and avatar to be as it appears on your Google profile, click 'Create a username' on the bottom right of your screen.
- Check the boxes to indicate what activities you want to share on your 'channel'.
- Click 'OK, I'm ready to continue'.

Note: the name that you choose will become the name of your YouTube channel and it will be viewable by everyone. YouTube usernames must be one word, with no spaces or special characters, so use capital letters to separate words, as upper and lower case letters are permitted. Once you have chosen a name, it cannot be changed, so consider it carefully and choose something that is easy for other people to remember or identify you by.

On the next screen, you may be asked to confirm your account via a text message or a telephone call. Finally, YouTube will send a verification email to the address you used to create the account. Click the link in that email to verify your account and then you can get started. Don't forget to customise your YouTube profile, to emphasise key information.

Complete every field that is applicable to your business in order to help people find your account on YouTube. The mandatory fields to fill out include your name, website URL, channel description (an idea of what people can expect from your YouTube videos) and hometown (location).

There are optional additional fields such as interests, books, movies and about me, which can either be completed or left blank. By taking a few minutes to fill them in, you will be able to give a human feel to your account and allow viewers to feel they know a little more about you. Generally, the more information you include, the better.

Making an Effective Video

Making a video is simple and if you don't have a camera, it can even be done from your phone; however, you should take into account the following:

- To attract people to read your book you would be best advised to make short videos about your topic, giving small amounts of free advice and information.
- Before you make a video, consider the type of image you wish to create. Whacky and casual can be great, but only if it fits in with your style.
- Always introduce yourself in a friendly manner.
- Tell the viewer what you are doing and where they can buy your book.
- Consider reading your blurb and definitely have a copy of your book on display.
- Read a chapter or extract/excerpt of your book.
- End with a call to action – in other words, send them to your site or tell them how they can find you on other social media sites.
- Have a specific goal in mind when creating a video.
- Consider having some appropriate background music.
- Add subtitles and annotations to your video.
- With a video in which you feature, your audience can feel like they are connecting with and getting to know you directly, in person, so show your human side.
- State why your book is different or interesting.
- Show people what they will get or how they will benefit by reading your book.
- Talk about your background or interests.
- Discuss how you came to write the book.
- Demonstrate that you know what you are talking about, thereby giving your audience a reason to come to you, buy your book, use your services.

- Only use images you own, so you don't run into copyright issues.
- Offer solutions to common problems and answers to frequently asked questions.

Don't read from a sheet of paper. Instead, create a list of bullet points stating the topics you wish to cover as a form of prompts, otherwise you will not look natural or as though you know your subject. Also, people will see you looking down or to one side in order to read an extract in front of you.

Driving Sales with YouTube

I wonder how many of you have landed yourself in hot water by sending a text or email, where the message you intended has been misconstrued ... The advantage of YouTube is that you can use tone and expression to convey your meaning.

It might mean coming out of your comfort zone to put yourself on show, but you can broadcast anything you want on YouTube. It can be a means of letting the world know about the products and services you offer, including a new book launch, how you develop characters, how you conduct research and preparation, places where you like to write, how you came to write, etc.

Consider some of the following:

- Conduct interviews and reviews.
- If you have written a children's book, consider reading an extract, like a sort of story time for children, in a chair in front of the fire.
- Consult with experts or people who have read your book for reviews, interviews and testimonials.
- Use keywords from your target audience to find and connect with them. The title of your book is not a keyword, as you will be starting out as an unknown entity. Instead, it could be the genre of your book or, if you are writing non-fiction, the niche area your book deals with.
- Build hype prior to and leading up to a book launch – otherwise known as book trailers.

- Offer a discount on your book if they quote a code you given in the video or a concession for a limited time period.

Don't forget, YouTube is visual and your book cover is also visual, so use it in your video. Experiment and have fun using YouTube. We remember our first video only too well and with practise, nerves soon disappear.

Pinterest

If a picture is worth a thousand words ... then Pinterest may be worth a thousand sales!

Co-founded by Ben Silbermann and Paul Sciarra in 2010, Pinterest initially operated out of a small apartment. As the name suggests, this site allows you to use pictures or images known as 'pins' as the focus to organise, discuss and spread ideas and interests.

It has been described as a pinboard-style social photo-sharing website that allows users to create and manage collections of images based on a theme. It is the latest craze on the Internet and it can be extremely addictive. It had achieved over 100 million users by December 2015 with most users under the age of 40.[4] It is said to be the third most popular way to share behind Facebook and Twitter. Only 47% of users log on weekly.[5]

Instead of operating like Facebook and Twitter, which rely on text to share information, Pinterest functions as a sort of online visually stimulating inspirational pinboard or bookmarking site. Because the majority of the traffic is female, if you are trying to target this audience, this site is the ideal platform.[6]

We think Pinterest is a useful platform on which to market your book in that it is a visual product and as such you can display an image of your book cover. If you have a great cover and a catchy title, it is a good platform to be seen on. Put simply, on Pinterest you organise your interests by subject titles known as boards, such as 'books worth reading', 'my favourite characters', etc. Your boards, where you collect your pins, generally represent a collection of clippings from magazines, printouts of things found online, quotations, fables, photographs and keepsakes that inspire creativity. These collections of images can be based on a theme and when you first open an account, Pinterest will suggest some from which to start. You can always add themes as you go along.

Once your images are pinned on your boards, if you click on the image it will take you to the website the image is attached to, once you have added the appropriate links, either to purchase the product or to find out more about it.

The Pinterest visual version of a social media platform enables you to do all sorts of things:

- Create a personal profile, using imagery to make it more personal.
- If you like a particular website or an idea, you can 'pin' it to your board.
- Use collections of displayed images as recommendations.
- Place 'Pin it' buttons on your website so that people can easily add a picture of your book cover to their profile. If users 'pin' your cover to their profile with a brief, optional description, it gives their followers the opportunity to buy your book based on their recommendation. To get the 'Pin it' button, go to <http://pinterest.com/about/goodies> and place it next to your Twitter and Facebook buttons.
- Add captions to your images and also links to the original article; you cannot currently add a link to one of your own images that you have uploaded.
- Display images that represent discounts on your book, such as coupons or vouchers.
- Follow groups or friends.
- Browse other pinboards for inspiration, 're-pin' images and 'like' photographs.

Like any other social networking site, you need to gain followers, who in turn 're-pin' your posts, in order to have any influence and gain visibility. The more 'likes' and 're-pins', the greater visibility your post will get, even becoming featured on Pinterest boards that are visible to the public; note that boards can be made secret or public.

Setting Up a Pinterest Account

To join, you have to request an invitation from the Pinterest home page or from an existing user, which will then ask you for your email address. It really is that simple!

- Go to <http://www.pinterest.com>.
- Click 'Join Pinterest'.
- Choose how you will sign up: e.g. via Facebook, Twitter or your email address.
- Enter a username (3–15 characters or numbers, but not spaces, symbols or punctuation), an email address and a password.
- Click 'Create Account'.

Bear in mind that it may take a few days for the request to be activated.

Adding Pins to Your Boards

It is very easy to add pins to your board. To upload a pin from your computer to one of your Pinterest boards, follow these instructions:

- Log into your Pinterest account.
- Click the 'Add' button on the right-hand side of your screen.
- Click the 'Upload a Pin' button.
- Click the 'Browse' button.
- Select the file you want to upload.
- Click 'Open' on the right-hand side of your screen at the bottom.
- Click the drop-down menu to select the board you want to post the pin to or create a new board.
- Add a description for your image in the field below the board name.
- Click the 'Pin it' button.

Adding Products to Your Boards

It is very easy to add images to your boards:

- Upload the Pinbox to your website toolbar from Pinterest.
- Go to your website or the store from where you want to pin your product.
- Click the Pinbox on your toolbar menu.

- Pinterest will open automatically on your screen and all your product images on that particular website page will appear.
- Pick the one you want to pin.
- Pinterest will prompt you which board you want to pin it to or you can create a new one by scrolling down on the categories.
- Add a description of the product to help people find your pin, of up to 500 words.
- Add the price after the description, which will be displayed in upper left-hand corner of the image.

Priced products will be placed on the gifts tab on the top of Pinterest's home page. Pinterest will automatically link to your site or product when a person clicks on it. It really is that simple.

Copyright and Pinterest

With each image you 'pin' there is the option to add text, a caption or a comment about that picture. The only thing you cannot do is add your own links to the images you upload. The user absorbs the copyright legalities, so ensure you own the content or have permission to use it if you are to avoid copyright issues.

Pinterest offers the facility for any website to install a piece of code so that when someone tries to 'pin' it, they get a message that says 'this website does not allow pinning'. While websites are responsible for installing this code, it does not override the copyright statements people have on their site.

Driving Sales with Pinterest

- Pinterest is a bit like window-shopping, in that the images you pin should entice people to look inside (metaphorically speaking).
- As well as images, you could post the first page or paragraph of your book and underneath include details of where it can be purchased.
- Add pins with price tags; by adding a price to your pin, you can direct users to your website to buy.

- Use it as a marketing tool, by posting an image of your book cover.
- Hold a contest, asking others to pin their own images or images of your book that you have created, where they choose their favourite and the one who gets the most engagement wins.
- Get fans to post their own images of them reading your book in various locations around the world.
- Offer to repin things for others, in return for them pinning your images.
- Share highlights of an event you have attended, on what you noticed or learned. Record things on camera, video recorder, etc.
- Use it like a catalogue of book titles and products you have produced.
- Run promotions and pin an exclusive discount code to the first few people who express an interest in perhaps signing up for your newsletter or joining an email list, thereby creating excitement, 'noise' or a 'buzz'.
- Perhaps offer a two-for-one, BOGOF – any strategy that encourages sales.
- Display images of printable coupons that can be redeemed on your website.
- Present insights about you, your book or company.
- If you are giving a certain percentage of your profits to charity or a good cause, use this as a marketing tool.
- Use your existing platforms and networks to drum up activity on your Pinterest boards.
- Know your market and remember that Pinterest is largely female-orientated.

Sourcing More Ideas for Pins

- Show behind-the-scenes images of your life as an author.
- With a children's book, you could add illustrations from your book.

- Add images of your characters, places, settings, etc.
- Show pictures that have inspired you to write or images representing favourite films, books or music.
- Create boards using themes, including events and beliefs, such as a 'Settings' board, where you can pin pictures of specific places or settings that might feature in your book.
- Providing you have their permission, you can pin pictures of staff or organisations, so people can put a face to the name of employees.
- Use it to collect research material for your next novel, such as landscapes, buildings, people, places, etc.
- Make an 'Ideas' board, where you capture images or photographs that motivate you to write or that inspire the story for your next book.
- Pin images of your preferred writing desk/room.
- Include a board where other people can post things about themselves, such as facial expressions, etc., whereby people can source ideas and become inspired to write.
- Add a price, so that it appears on Pinterest's gifts tab at the top of their homepage.
- Pin' images of your favourite writing implements.
- Have a 'Characters' board, based on characters in your stories.
- Add useful content, help and advice in the form of images.
- Pin a catchy slogan, quotation or strapline.
- Use images and photographs to illustrate how far you have come – your journey – like a start to finished/end product. In other words, show how your book has evolved through images. Share your ups and downs.
- Create a visual CV of your latest work.
- Share details about you and show your human side.
- Ask followers what they think by giving them options if you are making big decisions, whereby perhaps they can repin the ones they like.

- Post images of places where you have seen your book or, better still, create a travelog of where your book has been, countries and places it has visited, etc. Perhaps holding an 'around the world' competition with your book.

Remember, it doesn't always have to be a picture that you 'pin' – an image of displayed words can be just as effective.

Summary

Pinterest is a very different platform to the text-based options. Have fun experimenting with this platform as you learn its benefits and discover whether or not it is right for you and your book.

YouTube is your opportunity to engage with readers other than with the written word. It can be a very powerful marketing tool. If you are really uncomfortable in front of the camera, consider making a video using still images, such a photographs with music and or a recording of you speaking about your book.

As with other social media, these platforms can be time-consuming, so it is undoubtedly best to have a targeted approach:

- Decide who your target audience is.
- Establish the best places to contact and connect with them.
- Find out what sites, magazines, etc., they are using.
- Define the image and message you want to portray.
- Speak their language.
- If you decide to use the services of someone to assist you with social media, make sure you can trust them to only put out material you would approve of.

The great thing about social media is that you are no longer alone in what can be an otherwise isolating career choice: writing. Don't try to do it all at once – spend a couple of weeks at least learning each platform properly, before moving on to the next one, in order to be effective. In other words, become proficient in one at a time.

Key Points

- Make the most of your bio or profile and highlight your experience.

- Update your profile and experience regularly, to ensure it remains current.
- Only connect with people you know on LinkedIn.
- Use an image of yourself for your profile on LinkedIn.
- Avoid posting too many status updates on LinkedIn.
- Don't read from a sheet when making a video for YouTube.
- Avoid copyright issues.
- Use your time wisely and avoid the temptation to become addicted – remember: everything in moderation.
- Continue to work on your existing platforms.
- Avoid periods of complete inactivity.
- Learn each platform in full before trying a new one.

Next Steps

- Set up a LinkedIn account.
- Write a professional bio, providing as much detail as you can.
- Start following groups of interest.
- Consider setting up a group and/or company page on LinkedIn.
- Start building your network by connecting with people who share your interests.
- Write some recommendations and give endorsements.
- Participate in conversation threads that have already been started, preferably becoming the first to make a response.
- Set up a YouTube account.
- Start making some videos.
- Decide if you are going to try any other platforms, such as Pinterest.
- Create a Pinterest profile.
- Add pictures and images of your book.

Chapter Five – LinkedIn, YouTube and Pinterest

- Create some boards and start pinning content/material to them.
- Start following other Pinterest users.

Footnotes

1. See <http://press.linkedin.com/about> [accessed 23.12.15]
2. See <http://wersm.com/top-linkedin-facts-and-stats-infographic/> [accessed 23.12.15]
3. See <http://www.youtube.com/yt/press/en-GB/statistics.html> [accessed 23.12.15]
4. See <http://expandedramblings.com/index.php/pinterest-stats/> [accessed 23.12.15]
5. See <http://www.wired.com/2014/01/pinterest-more-popular-than-email/> [accessed 23.12.15]
6. See <http://expandedramblings.com/index.php/pintereststats/> [accessed 23.12.15]

Chapter Six – Websites

Many a small thing has been made large by the right kind of advertising.

Mark Twain

Introduction

Businesses, professionals, celebrities and in fact anyone looking to present a highly presentable image and connect with potential buyers need to have a website. If you don't have one yet, you could be missing out on a great opportunity to build your professional image.

First invented by Tim Berners-Lee, a website is a set of related web pages containing content (media) such as text, images, video, audio, etc. All publicly accessible websites collectively constitute the World Wide Web, created in 1990. It is free to use, although Internet providers and web hosting companies charge for using their services.

For most of us the idea of having to understand how websites work is enough to make us lose interest. But in reality, if you can find someone to create a simple WordPress site for you that you can update yourself, you don't really need much knowledge at all.

The purpose of this chapter is to explain how to use your site to market and sell your book, but before we begin we will explain a few of the most common phrases and words you will hear in relation to websites and the Internet.

- ☺ After all, even if someone is setting everything up for you, it is useful to understand the basics, so you don't feel like they are talking a foreign language.

Common terms include:

1. Hosting – in effect, hosting companies or web hosts, also known as ISPs (Internet Service Providers), rent you space on their computer (server) to hold your website files. For a website to exist and be accessible to consumers across the world, it must be on a Web server, which must always be connected to the Internet and running in the background.
2. HTTP (Hyper Text Transfer Protocol) – this refers to a server where a website is hosted and made accessible via the Internet.
3. LAN (private) local area network – this is what connects a group of computers in close proximity to each other, such as in an office building. It is used to transfer files and other objects across a privatised network on the Internet.
4. Uniform Resource Locator or URL – this is a global address of documents and pages on the World Wide Web.
5. Domain name – this is your URL extension; for example, <http://www.personalheights.com>.
6. HTML text (Hypertext Mark-up Language) – the name of the code in which websites are written.
7. Search engine optimization (SEO) – this is the process of obtaining organic traffic (visitors) to your website. It is done by improving the ranking of your website in search engine results without using paid advertising.

Custom-Built Websites

Websites don't have to be complex – a simple three-page site will be enough. Many people worry about constantly paying a webmaster for updates and amendments, but if you have a WordPress site, your web designer can set you up as an author, which means you can do simple updates for yourself.

Service providers offering simple, user-friendly sites are freeley available for a small outlay. For a basic website all you need is three pages:

- Home page – containing information about your book, including images and a 'buy' button linking to either Amazon or your publisher's website.

Chapter Six – Websites

- Bio page – containing information about you, with a form to allow interested parties to contact you.
- A built-in blog.

Consider what additional facilities you require such as shopping carts linked directly to your PayPal account, which may incur an additional fee. You may also decide to incorporate buttons to allow people to connect directly with your Twitter and Facebook accounts, so that you can share your content between the various social media platforms. You could even create your own using a service such as WordPress. Take into consideration, whether you want to post blogs and maintain the site yourself going forward, in which case building your own WordPress site may be your best option.

Selling Through Your Site

If you wish to sell your book direct from your site, you will need a merchant's account or a PayPal account. A merchant account is a type of bank account that allows businesses to accept payments via payment cards, typically debit or credit cards. PayPal is one of the best and most trusted organisations to make a secure monitory transaction. Remember, if you choose this method you will be responsible for the distribution of your book/s, so you may decide to send customers to Amazon or your publisher's website, instead.

Domain Names

Having the right domain name can rank your website higher on search engines like Google and high website rankings on Google means free traffic. It is important to ensure your domain name is relevant, for example:

- The title of your novel or self-help, how-to or non-fiction book; this option is limiting if you plan to write more than one book.
- Words relating to the subject of your book. For example, financial planning, hypnobirthing, etc.
- Alternatively you can use your own name for example: Rebeccarichmond.com

Your web designer will usually register the name for you as part of their service. But in order to register a domain name yourself, you will need to visit a domain registrar site like <http://www.godaddy.com>, which has a very simple process for registering names. It should be noted that you are not buying the domain name but are simply renting it for a period of time, such as twelve months or two years, and it will need to be renewed if you don't want to lose it.

Once you have chosen a domain registrar service, if you type in your preferred domain name – e.g., <http://www.personalheights.com> – and the URL extension '.com' has been taken, you will be offered alternative suggestions and variants of this that are available. Try different extensions, such as '.com' or '.net', or add hyphens or numbers. It should be noted here that very few people search for a business name. Instead, they type in keywords around it, such as:

- authors in Shropshire
- writing circles in Kent
- literary reviews in the UK
- write a novel/book
- overcome insomnia
- manage chronic pain/stress

Therefore, your domain name should also include keywords, such as 'shropshireauthor' or 'scifibookauthor'. Some examples of author websites include:

- <http://www.lindsaypritchardauthor.com>
- <http://www.daaubreyauthor.com>, and
- <http://www.ajmarshallauthor.com>

In these cases, the author's name was already taken, so we adapted it and included the keyword 'author'. This will also help people searching on the Internet, as it will enable them to determine whether or not they have found the right person/site.

Perhaps the biggest development for 2014 on the Internet in twenty years is the creation of 1,000 plus domain name extensions. This could now mean that extensions such as .clothing, .guru, .plumbing, .luxury, .build, .bike, geared to specific audiences, will become available.

Whilst you cannot always get the exact name you want, it is worth investing in and registering a good name. When buying a website, we would suggest the following order of preference for extensions to a domain name:

- domain name with the extension '.com.' does not specify a country and is particularly useful if you wish to engage with the US market
- domain name with the extension '.co.uk' if you are in the UK
- domain name with the extension '.org.uk' (which ranks just as well)
- exact keyword first plus suffix, e.g. review.information or review.guide
- exact keyword with hyphens and the extention '.co.uk' or '.com' (e.g. <http://www.how-to-write-a-novel.co.uk> or <http://www.book-marketing.com>)
- exact keyword with hyphens and '.org'
- domain name plus the extension '.net'.

Website Content

Although having a well-designed site and choosing the right images and banner are important, the quality of the content is more so, as this is how people will decide if they like your writing style and if they are interested enough to want to read a full novel. If you are unsure what style your site should have, browse the Net and look at other sites to get ideas for yours.

- ☺ By this we mean the style, layout and overall feel, rather than plagiarising the content.

As a general guideline, we would recommend you consider the following when building your website:

- Ensure it is easy to navigate.
- Decide where you want your tabs to appear. Do you want them to appear across the top or down the side of the screen? Do you want to include drop-down boxes, where the user can hover over a tab and more tabs appear?
- To convey your message and for emphasis, use lots of displayed and coloured text, different font sizes, italics, bold, underline, capitalisation, etc.

- Consider what colours you do or don't want included in the design of your website.
- Include images and logos to break up your text; but only use ones that support your content and that you own.
- Don't overcomplicate your message. People's attention span and time are short, so convey your message succinctly. Aim to delivery your message within the space of one screen, so that users don't have to scroll down.
- Use bullet points.
- Adopt short sentences and paragraphs.
- Make good use of keywords in the main body of the text on your website, ensuring that these are highlighted in some way.
- If you have a blog, carefully consider the categories you want to incorporate, based on your subject matter. For example, featured authors, grammar, characters, plot development, author's desk, coming soon, etc.
- A sure way to get your site downgraded or removed from search results is to duplicate content when describing you, your products and services. Utilise alternative mediums, such as slide presentations and videos, in which to present the information instead.
- Make sure your content can be viewed on mobile devices and smartphones.

How to Use a Website to Your Advantage

There are many advantages to having a website. You can use it to:

- Tell people about your background.
- Sell your books through it.
- Allow people to contact you with their queries.
- Display excerpts from each book, if you have written more than one.
- Run competitions, whereby those who answer a question are entered into a prize draw to win a copy of your book/s.
- Engage with your audience though your blog.
- Link to relevant sites.

Don't forget to support all your retailers by linking to several places where people can buy your book/s, giving your fans the option to purchase your book from their favourite retailer.

Instead of one-way interruption, Web marketing is about delivering useful content at just the precise moment a buyer needs it.
David Meerman Scott

There are many different aspects to marketing a book and different techniques apply, depending on whether or not your book is non-fiction or a novel:

Using a Website to Market Non-Fiction/Self-Help Books

- Explain why your book is going to help your reader, perhaps by making their life better in some way or by providing a new insight on a topic of interest to them.
- Repeat the message so it is re enforced in their minds.
- Think carefully about your wording and use terminology they will understand.
- If it is a self-help book, talk about the difficulties they may currently have and/or the improvements they can expect to experience from using your techniques or information.
- If someone has bought your book, ask them to write a testimonial or review. Always seek their permission prior to including it on your website.
- If possible, offer information for free. For example, you could give away the first chapter of your book or some related information. Whatever you decide to give away, it needs to add value and be a quality item, as people may judge your book on the quality of the free material.
- Consider offering no-risk, money-back guarantees. If you do this, you risk customers coming back after a certain period of time, such as ten or thirty days, for a refund and you have to be prepared to honour this. However, if your book is great, people will be less likely to do so.
- Include a time-limited offer, such as: take advantage of this now to avoid disappointment; limited number available at this price ...

- Make an instant download available, for those who don't want to wait, so they can get it within seconds. Ensure that people are clear that it isn't or book/eBook they are getting but a downloadable PDF.
- Give your contact information. At the very least, you should provide an email address. People want to know that they can get hold of you.

Using a Website to Market Fiction Books

Your website can be far more than just a page that gives details of your author bio and a synopsis of your book. It can be used to engage with your readers and encourage them to read your future novels by giving them excerpts prior to publication. Other things it can be used for include the following:

- If you have written a children's book, make it interactive, where readers can download things like a word search or pictures that they can colour in.
- Construct a game whereby one of your characters has to find a way out of a maze, etc.
- Include a page introducing your characters, so your readers can get to know them.
- Build in a Q&A.
- Incorporate a page with images of scenes and settings.
- Create a puzzle of missing/jumbled letters of the alphabet that they can use to form a word related to something in your book.
- Give prompts; e.g. draw what you think someone or something would look like. You could even incorporate this idea as a competition.
- Post details of events and signings you are running or attending.
- Include an inspiration or work-in-progress page.
- Blog about your latest work in progress.
- Offer soft toys or upsell other products related to your book such as postcards, posters, toys, pens, T-shirts, etc.

- Enable comments on your blog so that you can engage with your readers.

The downside of allowing people to comment on your posts is that it can encourage spam. However, you are able to moderate these and if you are getting lots, while it may be annoying, it means your site is being found, in which case well done and keep up the good work. ☺

Search Engine Optimization (SEO)

The methods of getting your site to rank highly in search engine results like Google change frequently. Google aim to stop people beating the system, whereby sites rank highly but the quality of the site and the information they contain is poor. In effect, Google is always looking to improve both content and how they deliver the information people search for.

To improve your site's ranking it requires planning and modifications to the coding and displayed content. Unless you have a very good understanding of the code in which your website is written, it is best to employ the services of a web builder to optimise your code. However, there are things you can do yourself to improve your ranking:

- Use keywords within the main body of your text.
- Ensure that the information within your pages is relevant.
- Don't duplicate content.
- Obtain links with other quality sites – in particular, authority sites, which tend to have extensions '.edu' or '.gov'.
- Never link to poor quality sites, even if you are offered an incentive.
- Don't link to sites that are not relevant to your topic or genre.
- Populate your site with other forms of data such as videos, voice recordings and images.
- Add new information on a regular basis.
- Use meta tags.

Improving your ranking can take time; however, it will be easier if you target a tight niche, with less competition. For example, it will be much harder to get on the first page of Google if you are competing on a very popular keyword such romance, which delivers about 380 million results!

Login Pages

Consider having a login page – otherwise known as a 'squeeze' page, catch page or 'login box'. This will enable you to capture names, email addresses, telephone numbers, etc., of visitors to your site. You can then use this information at a later date to connect with your authors and thereby promote your book. The downside of this is that it can deter visitors to your site, in that if it is necessary to supply contact details in order to be allowed access to the content on your site, they may leave your site without even logging on.

If you decide to create a squeeze page, avoid making your visitors complete lengthy forms and give some quality information that they can see without registering. The benefit of this is that if they like the free information, it will inspire them to register.

Shortening URLs

Some URLs can be hundreds of characters long using complex character patterns, making them cumbersome to use. As Twitter and other instant-messaging services limit the number of characters a message can carry, it can be useful to shorten your URL, thereby avoiding violating constraints. See the section on using SocialOomph for Twitter for details on how they tackle this.

Fortunately, URLs can be made substantially shorter in length and still direct the user to the required page. There are plenty of sites out there that shorten URLs and the one we use is Google <http://goo.gl/>. An example of a shortened link would be as follows:

- Full link: <http://www.personalheights.com/book-coaching/>
- Shortened link: <http://goo.gl/FGtBDV>

However, while they may be more convenient, with a shortened URL, the user cannot determine where they are actually going to be sent and so they may be reluctant to click the link on this basis. It really comes down to personal preference as to whether or not you use shortened URLs.

Meta Tags

Meta tags are used to provide information about a web page for the benefit of search engines and website users. Otherwise known as title tags, at a suggested maximum of seventy characters long, they enable people and search engines to determine what a page is about, encouraging or discouraging people to a website when shown in search results.[1]

While meta tags are now regarded as old school and the Google algorithms have downgraded them, they are still important, in addition to the meta description, which work just like tags, in that you can paste keywords in this space.

Meta description tags are displayed in search engine results pages and they appear beneath the title tag. Good descriptions can improve click-through rates. While using relevant keywords is important, it is also key to use a variety of words and phrases; although they should not be repeated too often, if you don't want your site downgraded.

Ideally, the title tag should contain important keywords that are page related and content descriptive, using pipes (|) rather than commas or other punctuation to separate keywords. In effect, the pipe means 'or'. For instance: if you had the URL <http://www.personal/heights.com/what-do-you-expect-from-coaching> it tells us that this article answers the question 'What do you expect from a coaching?'. Google will display this as: What do you expect from a coaching?|Personal Heights. Keywords are exactly what they state – words, not sentences – so omit small words like and, to, but, etc.

People like articles that give information. They want to see titles that give:

- tips
- answers to queries
- help
- advice
- solutions

Other popular ideas include:

- Five Things You Must Know ...
- Top Ten ...
- Three Unmissable Techniques ...

Anything that whets their appetite and creates intrigue.

Important things to remember about title tags:

- They should be short, simple and to the point, using a maximum of seventy characters, including spaces.

- Use optimised keywords in your title tag that are descriptive to the content on the page.
- Omit short extra words such as 'and', 'but', etc. If you need to use the word 'and', type '&' instead so that Google doesn't confuse it with searching for two separate things.
- Use pipes (|) to separate important keyword phrases (no commas, dashes, underscores, etc., unless the keyword is written that way).
- Include your company name at the end of a title tag, unless it is part of the important keywords.
- Consider categorising title tags, e.g. fiction, self-help, non-fiction; for example My Guide books | self-help | Personal Heights Coaching.
- Title tags should be different for each page.
- Avoid duplicate content as search engines downgrade sites that are filled with repetitive material.

RSS (Really Simple Syndication)

This feature enables users to subscribe to a certain site or feed in order to retrieve relevant and up-to-date information, which they can read at their own leisure. It is a means of distributing content from an online publisher to Internet users. In effect, it enables people to keep track of their favourite websites.

Put simply, RSS selects the latest headlines from different websites you are subscribing to and it then pushes those headlines/text files to your computer. The advantage of this is that instead of having to visit several different websites to retrieve information you are interested in – such as blogs, weather, writing advice, social media techniques, etc. – you only need to go to one screen, where it will be listed on a single window. With this feature, it is no longer necessary to 'bookmark' websites in your browser and manually return to them on a regular basis to see what has been added.

The RSS feed symbol is a button or icon that is usually orange that appears on each site that reads 'RSS'. It looks like a wireless symbol tipped on its side (a dot with two curved lines above it, extending to the right).

If you want to start reading sites via RSS, get yourself an RSS feed reader such as AOL Reader, Awasu, Digg Reader, Feedly, intraVnews, Mozilla Thunderbird, RSS Bandit, RSS Bot, SharpReader, Squeet, amongst others.

You can then use the information you read as inspiration for articles and blogs of your own. By having an RSS button on your site, your readers can add your site to their reading list, so they can return to your content easily.

Google Overview

The Google market is not as big in the US as it is in the UK, but it is still a major player. In the US, the search engines Yahoo and Microsoft's Bing are more dominant, which have merged their search results to compete with Google. Google displays sites it believes are authoritative and relevant and when ranking sites, they are looking at:

- Website appearance.
- User experience.
- Facebook and Twitter activity (or other social media platforms).
- How long people spend on the site and whether or not people click straight out of a site; providing good content keeps people on your site so that you don't get a high bounce rate.
- Low click-through rates, where a website is listed on a search result but consistently not picked.
- Google Chrome enables you to block sites from results if they weren't relevant to your search.
- Page content.
- Duplicate content.
- Relevancy of content.
- Words used.
- Optimised keywords.
- Fresh content that is updated constantly.

- Authority, based on the number and quality of other pages linking to the pages they show. In other words, good links; links act like votes.
- Adverts that add value to a site.

The reason they have revised their practises is to combat spam sites.

Paid Advertising on Google

Google offer a facility called pay-per-click advertising, whereby every time someone clicks on a site, the site owner pays a fee. The advantage of this is that you can set the budget, spending as little or as much as you want, and you can use targeted keywords and phrases.

Although this is great for getting instant traffic to your website, it can work out quite expensive. With Google Adwords, for example, you can pay significant amounts of money for one click alone and even then, there is no guarantee that that person will go on to buy anything or indeed stay on your site. We would never advocate the use of this type of advertising for low-income products. You really need a product in excess of £150 to make it worthwhile investing in.

> Half the money I spend on advertising is wasted, and the problem is I do not know which half.
>
> Lord Leverhulme

Google Plus (+)

Google+ was launched in June 2011 and had in excess of 2.2 billion registered users 2015, according to Business Insider UK; although only 9 per cent of these actively post public content.[2] Growing in popularity, Google+ will increase blog traffic, influence your site result on search engines and may increase the chances of people clicking onto your site.

A +1 recommendation from someone is a signal to Google proving that your content is relevant and quality. You can add this button to your website, to enable people to recommend your content, thereby driving traffic to your blog.

A strong Google+ profile improves search results. When creating your profile, under your name you can provide a brief description of yourself. Ensure that the wording you choose is short and concise, so that the information fits in the entire line, without ellipses signifying that the text continues.

Google Options

In the 'About' section of your 'Profile', you can add links to your website and other social media sites, so that people can find you elsewhere online. At the bottom of the 'About' page you need to ensure that in profile discovery 'Links' at the bottom of the screen, your profile is made visible or public in searches in order for people to be able to find you. There is also a box where you can include a small photograph of yourself and a banner.

Like Facebook, there is the ability to create a business page. And like Twitter, Google+ uses hashtags (#) to help sort information and allow people to search for posts on a particular topic. See the chapter on Twitter for more information on hashtags; although hashtags are not exclusive to Twitter and are a great way to pull in relevant audiences searching for certain things or topics. A good way to get yourself noticed is if you can link your message with an existing trending topic. Go to <http://www.google.co.uk/trends/> or <http://www.google.co.uk/trends/hottrends> to explore trends and find out what topics are currently 'hot'.

In Google+ you can create what is known as circles. This is a means of categorising people online; for instance, organising people into groups such as family, personal, business, etc. Anything you post can then be streamed to reach or target a specific circle, so that not all your circles see all of your posts and thereby receive only relevant information.

> *What makes content engaging is relevancy. You need to connect the contact information with the content information.*
>
> *Gail Goodman*

Once you have started creating circles, you can go to the top right of your screen and click on your name with the plus sign (+) against it. From there, a new screen will appear. In the top left of the screen under the 'home' button with a picture of a house against it, you can then view 'what's hot', which will show you what is hot within your circles and also what is trending on Google+.

Google Alerts is a content change detection and notification service that automatically monitors and notifies users when new content on the Internet matches a search result selected by the user. You can set up 'alerts' so that you are notified via email whenever someone:

- writes your name
- posts an article you might be interested in
- mentions your book
- posts something on Twitter
- mentions your Twitter handle or site URL
- posts on topics you are interested in, etc.,

in accordance with the search terms or queries you have specified, whenever something new or relevant is posted.

Using this feature, you can start to connect with people in your niche and also your fans, whenever topics you have set to receive pop up online.

Summary

In a global market, whether you are in business or an author, having a Web presence is essential, unless you are only looking to conduct business in a very local area. Even then, most people assume that if you don't have a website, you are not a professional author.

So whether you are looking for customers locally or in a wider market, a website is the ideal place to connect with potential customers, particularly if you are able to write an interesting blog on a regular basis.

Key Points

- Capture people's email addresses, where people sign up to receive something for free, by adding a login/squeeze page to your website.
- Check out the size of your market and the level of competition. If competition is high, consider focusing on a smaller niche.
- Consider what other products you can sell alongside your book.
- Consider aiming for a smaller niche market.
- Ensure you have a web presence.
- Look at other exciting websites and consider what features or layouts you like the feel of, on which to model yours.

- Only consider paid advertising if you have a high-income product.
- Use keywords and meta descriptions to your advantage.
- Create a website page for each product, in order for Google to rank it.
- Avoid duplicate content.
- Deliver fresh content and blog on a regular basis.
- Consider your marketing strategies carefully, in accordance with whether you have written a fiction or a non-fiction book.
- Link to several retailers where people can buy your book.
- Convey ideas succinctly and avoid a long, rambling sentences; bullet points can be useful.
- Repeat your message often.
- Ensure your content can be viewed on mobile devices and smartphones.
- Enable comments so you can engage with your readers.
- Make full use of shortening URLs.
- Get an RSS reader.

Next Steps

- Set up a Google+ account.
- Choose a good domain name.
- Find a web designer and get them to build a website for you or build one of your own.
- Look at other things you can write, tweet, post and pin about.
- Consider how many pages you want your website to contain.
- Start following other sites and blogs using your reader and RSS feature.
- Add a 'share it' button to your website.
- Pay particular attention to delivering relevant content that is information rich.

- Consider the look and feel of your website.
- Write articles that give information, whets the appetite and creates intrigue.

Footnotes

1. It is currently thought that it can be slightly less than 70 characters.
2. See <http://uk.businessinsider.com/google-active-users-2015-1> [accessed 23.12.15]

Chapter Seven – Blogging and Articles

We're at the point now where the challenge isn't how to communicate effectively with e-mail, it's ensuring that you spend your time on the e-mail that matters most.

Bill Gates

Introduction

We believe the most effective way to market your book online is to have website of your own where you can blog. From this website you can then sell your book, products and services, if you have them or plan to develop them. Websites are covered in detail in Chapter Six. In this chapter we hope to inspire you to begin blogging either through your website or one of the other platforms available.

What is Blogging?

The word 'blog' stands for 'web log'. Blogs have been around for about ten years and are effectively online diaries, typically displayed in reverse chronological order so the most recent post appears first. They are usually posted by a single individual or group and are often themed on topics or categories. A blog is a way of building social relations with readers of the blog and other bloggers, creating a sort of community.

Anyone can set one up, that's the easy part, and there are three ways to do this:

1. You can use one of the sites that offer free blogging. For example: WordPress, LiveJournal and Blogger, amongst others. Sites like these will offer you a free blog site with its own address, to become <http://www.nameofmyblog.com>, for

example. This is the address you give friends and prospective readers who might want to take a look. Once you have set up your blog you can then post entries whenever you wish.

They are simple to set up. All you need to do is enter your details where it says 'create account' and off you go ... it really is that simple! ☺ The downside of using one of the free blogs as opposed to having your own site is that you cannot sell your book from these pages.

Once your account has been created you will be taken to a page that allows you to complete a profile and tell readers about yourself. Then you can begin the fun part! You will have the facility to upload any information you wish to share such as articles, blogs, videos, pictures. When you are ready to share this information with the world it could not be easier – simply click the publish button. ☺ Just make sure you own the copyright.

You will also be given the option of allowing people to comment on your posts. Good blogs are interactive, but it is entirely down to personal preference as to whether or not you want people to comment. While allowing people to post can create a buzz, particularly if you are blogging on a controversial subject, you must also be prepared for some blunt or negative comments. Fortunately, you do have the option to check comments before they are shown or displayed on your blog and made public.

If you receive negative comments, don't become disheartened. It is only one person's opinion and it may be that their opinion isn't one you would value anyway. It is their perception of the world and you don't have to let it influence you in any way.

Coaching Tip:

Perception is how we perceive events that happen around us and our perception of something is based on the beliefs and values that we have been forming since we were born. This is why two people can witness exactly the same event and have a completely different view on it.

In addition to this, your mood and emotions on a particular day can change your perception of something. By this we mean that something that may make you laugh while in a

Chapter Seven – Blogging and Articles

good mood enjoying a day out with friends could make you want to scream if you are feeling down.

Remember, you don't have to take on someone else's perception of something. Be brave and form your own opinions. Believe in yourself.

You can always use bad publicity to your advantage, by reposting it and inviting comments. In most cases you will find that people are prepared to argue the case on your behalf. Remember, there is always someone out there who will try to discredit your work. But you don't have to take it on board; unless you believe it will help you improve your next book.

2. You can apply to some of the established blogging sites to become a guest blogger. Again, you can't sell from these sites. Some examples of popular ones are:

   Masquerade Crew:
   (<http://www.masqueradecrew.blogspot.com>)
   Writing.ie:
   (<http://www.writing.ie/guest-blogs/>)
   GalleyCat:
   (<http://www.adweek.com/galleycat/>)

   However, when you are submitting articles to these and other sites, it needs to be relevant to both yours and their market.

3. The advantage of having your own website is that you can sell from it. As we have already stated, there are plenty of service providers offering reasonably priced custom-built websites with blog.

Important Points About Blogging

- People won't thank you if your blog is one long sales pitch. Even though it is an opportunity to reach out to customers, this type of marketing is known as spamming and you will lose the trust of your followers or be ignored.
- Think of something interesting or entertaining to say each time you blog.
- Keep your blog focused around your topic. For example, if people have subscribed to a blog about

weight training and then you post blogs about flower arranging, they may unsubscribe. Likewise, if you have written a historical romance and start blogging about rugby, don't be surprised if you lose subscribers.
- Choose something current to write about.
- Respond to comments quickly and professionally.
- Include links to your social media platforms in your blogs.
- Consider how often you are going to post a blog. We would recommend you blog at regular intervals, either weekly, fortnightly or monthly. However, the optimum blogging rate is a minimum of once a week.
- Your blog has to be well written and all entries should be checked for grammar, punctuation and spelling, as your reputation is at stake here.
- Between 300 and 500 words is the optimum length. People are not looking for a book in an article.
- Your blog needs to contain more in-depth content with more detailed information.
- Short sentences are better than long ones. Consider using bullet points rather than long, rambling sentences and paragraphs.
- Mention your subject as often as possible without labouring the point.
- State the main point of your blog/article in your first paragraph to help your blog get listed prominently on the search engines.
- In your blog there will be a section for 'tags' – words you would associate with your blog – which also help it come up in searches; this is similar to keywords.
- Ensure you complete your meta data or description, which describes and gives information about what you have written.
- Write in the same style as your book, so people can get used to your writing and hopefully decide to read more of your work.
- Add keywords in italics, bold and underline for each keyword, three times. Keywords are the words that

you believe best depict what your blog is about and will help search engines find it. For example, if your blog is about orcas in Canada, your keywords may be orca, Canada and killer whale.
- Consider adding an author bio at the end of your article.
- Word of caution: you should only use images and videos that you own to avoid copyright issues.
- Steer clear of contentious or controversial subjects that may lead to legal complications such as defamation or liability, or topics concerning politically sensitive areas.
- Your blogs should be civil, and your conduct and views around what is acceptable behaviour should be self- regulated. Abusive comments have no place on a blog and it is you who is responsible for the content.
- If you are having a bad day, that might not be the best day to post. If you recognise that you are feel low or irritable, by all means prepare the post, but don't publish until you are in a more neutral frame of mind.

Avoid solely concentrating on the text – images, slide presentations, videos and photographs are also important. However, you still need text so the search engine spiders can evaluate your content as a whole, to increase the chances of your blog coming up in search engine results. Yes, we did say spiders!

☺ Any arachnophobes can stop screaming – we don't mean the eight-legged kind.

In brief, in order for a search engine to tell the web browser where a file or document is, it must be found. The World Wide Web contains literally hundreds of millions of web pages and is still growing. So a search engine (e.g. Google) utilises special software robots, called spiders, to build lists of words found on websites. When a spider is building its lists, the process is known as Web Crawling. The starting point is generally lists of heavily used servers and most popular pages. The spider will begin with a popular site, indexing the words on its pages and following every link found within the site. Using this method, the 'spidering' system quickly spreads out across the most widely used portions of the Web.

Continue to add content to your blog or website each week. If you can't manage weekly, then monthly is still better than not at all. Regardless of how frequently you post, the content must be unique each time. Search engines like Google favour updated sites and fresh content. As with any blog, it takes time to become popular and to build a loyal following, so don't give up if it doesn't deliver results straight away.

When you're ready to quit, you're closer than you think
Bob Parsons

If you are going to release a blog every week, bear in mind that you will need a total of fifty-two articles over the course of a year. Not all of these have to be your own material. You can always invite people to become guest bloggers.

Guest Blogging

This is where you write an article or blog to be posted on someone else's site. Submitting guest blogs to someone else's site can be a useful tool because if they have lots of visitors, it will get your name out there.

If you are guest blogging:

- Contact whoever you are going to feature as a guest blogger for and advise them in advance what subject you propose to write about and how long the said article will be.
- Ask if you can post external links. If not, check if you can include an author bio and tell people about yourself.
- See if they have a particular house style they want you to follow that makes the articles uniform.
- It is not fair to expect whoever you are writing for to check, edit and alter your article when they aren't being paid anything to do so and are providing this service for free. Remember that it is not just your reputation at stake here.
- Make your article relevant to their site and the type of readership they might be targeting.
- Bear in mind that if it is not of a good enough quality, your submission may be rejected.

- Post links on your social media sites to the article in order to gain more/new traffic.
- Be selective when considering who you are going to write guest blogs for. For instance, there is no point posting an article about a character in your book who is a knitting granny on a football club site, unless of course she proposes to knit the team scarves and upsell them ...

Get people talking about your website or blog by commenting on other blogs and forums. Go to Q & A sites and actively engage with people, asking and answering queries. It is helpful if you can be one of the first to comment, rather than coming in later, when thirty other people have already left comments.

Articles

Gain readers and perfect your article writing skills by producing articles and material for newspapers, magazines, e-zines (online magazines), local radio stations, blogs, tweets, posts, etc. Ensure the copies you submit are 'clean', in that they should be well written, spellchecked and edited; this should be the foundation of all of your writing.

If you are going to submit an article to an online e-zine, check their guidelines for submission. Many insist that the article is unique and others might state that it mustn't contain links; in other words, you cannot add a link for someone to view your website or product on an external site. Each time someone shares an article using the Twitter button, for example, it keeps a record or tally of the number of times the content has been shared, giving an indication of how well it has been received.

Aim your writing at your market – people interested in a particular topic or a targeted demographic – for example, pregnant women. Don't merely try to impress or intimidate non-specialists with pretentious, stuffy language. Articles should not be used as an opportunity to demonstrate your grasp of the English language. Bring old content to life by recycling your articles, short stories or posts and reworking them with fresh eyes and latest developments.

Stick to topics you enjoy and that interest you. If you are bored with your work or struggling to find content, it will show in your writing.

Online Articles and Keywords

A keyword or phrase is simply the words or phrase typed into the search box of Google, Bing or other search engine in order to find information, etc. For example, if you are searching for a takeaway in a particular town you might type: Indian takeaway Chester.

When writing an <u>article</u> for ezines, websites or blogs, you will need to add a title, a description and keywords for each **article**. The *article* title is probably the most critical part. For blogs, you will also need to highlight your keyword or keyword phrase three times within the main body of the <u>article</u>: once in bold, once in italics and once in underline, as demonstrated with the word '*article*' in this paragraph. Ensure your keyword appears at different points within your **article** and not always at the start or end of a sentence or paragraph.

A simple way to find keywords your potential readers might use is to use Google's keyword search. This tool is designed to help you if you are creating a Google ad but can be very useful when researching your market.

When you enter words or phrases that are related to your product or service in the Google Keyword Tool, keyword ideas that are related to your terms are displayed. The Keyword Tool can help you find keywords that you might not even have thought of. For example, if you conduct a search on 'white chocolate', you might see keywords displayed such as 'white chocolate', 'candy bars', 'organic white chocolate bars' or 'white chocolate cake'.

Use the Keyword Tool by starting with broad keywords and terms and then narrow the search, getting more specific each time. For example, you might want to start searching on the keyword 'chocolate' and then 'milk chocolate' and 'dark chocolate'. Experimenting will produce more keyword ideas and increase the likelihood of you coming up with something suitable.

When you search for keyword ideas, you might see keywords that don't really apply to your book or business. You can add these as negative keywords, so that it doesn't bring them up again next time.

> *You can have brilliant ideas, but if you cannot get them across, your ideas will not get you anywhere.*
>
> Lee Lacocca

Getting someone to select your article over others that appear in the search results usually comes down to the title and the first few lines. Your title can be something simple – as this may set you apart from the other results on the search engine page – or you can create intrigue. For example, 'Ten Things You Need to Know About When ...' Titles like this work because our natural curiosity makes us wonder if we know all ten, and if the ten we know are the same ten you have listed.

Create a file where you keep article or short story titles to use at a later date. Having a list of titles can prompt you when you get writer's block, so that you can choose one to write that you feel most comfortable and inspired with.

> **Coaching Tip:**
>
> If you are struggling to find content and you find you have writer's block, try writing for just five minutes instead of half an hour. You never know, you may even find that your creative side comes out, you lose track of time and before you know it, you have an article to be proud of.
>
> Failing that, you could always try taking a break and doing something completely different.
>
> If all else fails, try writing:
> - another day
> - about something completely different
> - at a different time of day
> - in a different place.
>
> For instance, you might find you are more creative when working outside or looking out over a busy street or the park.
>
> Try jotting down ideas on a piece of paper or starting articles as and when you get inspiration. You can always come back to them when you have more detail to add.

Articles and Accuracy

Always proofread your articles several times because if your articles are littered with mistakes, it will bring into doubt the rest of your work.

Overfamiliarity can be a problem, so if you can find a third party to check your work, all the better. Failing that, put it aside for a few days and come back to it refreshed.

Facts and figures should be accurate and your article should address something current, that people are interested in. Keep an eye out for factual statements that are clearly wrong, e.g. Stockholm being the capital of Norway, or *The War of the Worlds* written by Charles Dickens. If you get it wrong, you may even find that it affects future submissions you may wish to write.

There will always be someone out there who is keen to disprove facts and figures, so you need to make note of the source if you are quoting them. If your material was sourced from the Internet, you will need to provide details of the date you accessed the information or data. For example <http://www.personalheights.com/blog> [accessed 31 January 20XX]. It is also a good idea to save or print a hard copy for future reference, as material on the Internet is not available forever and you might need to refer to it at a later date.

Short Stories

Short stories are a great way to give people an insight into your writing. However, you should bear in mind that writing a short story is very different to writing a novel. In a short story, there is no time for long, descriptive passages. Neither can you afford to include details such as family background. Remember, less is more. Even if it is a gentle tale of romance, every word has to count and move the story along.

Before submitting your short story for consideration, ensure you have read and complied with all submission requirements. As with articles, it is vital that any submission has been properly edited as mistakes can ruin your reputation before your career even gets off the ground.

Sourcing Ideas for Articles or Short Stories Externally

There is great potential for new material every day all around us, but if you have written a book about a particular topic, you should stick to that topic as much as possible. You might write a brilliant article or for an e-zine about organic gardening that receives rave reviews, but if your book is about how to make a fortune selling retro clothing on the Internet, your article is hardly likely to attract readers who will buy your book. You would be better writing an article about how to put together a retro outfit on a budget.

Likewise, if you write a short story for *The People's Friend* that is a heart-warming and gentle tale of a couple reunited after a separation of fifty years, although it may be a great success, the readers of this publication will not be your target audience if the novel you have written is a graphic thriller with explicit sex scenes and violence.

However, even though your articles or stories should always be in a similar vein to your book, you can still seek additional ideas and inspiration around this topic. Here are some great ways:

- Look in the press for current issues relating to your topic and then write articles or stories about the changes, developments or news.
- Observe beyond your immediate surroundings; for example, different cultures or spectres of society that you wouldn't normally have a connection with or that are not directly associated with your topic or genre.
- Look at posters, paintings and photographs with a curious mindset. Ask yourself what story this image could be portraying. If you have not tried this before, give it a go – it can be a great source of inspiration for short stories and even novels.
- If you are traveling on public transport, flying or sitting in a cafe, become a people watcher and invent stories around the people you see. Recently, when checking in to board a cruise, as well of lots of other individuals, there was a married couple who were dressed as a skunk and a crocodile, and a pair of identical twins, who were in their fifties who were dressed identically, even down to their jewellery. I came up with some stories around these characters, but you will have to wait to read about them. ☺
- Ask questions and try to see things from a different perspective or another's viewpoint.
- Try to include something new, that people might not already know, to create intrigue.
- Create a twist on a headline.
- Condense articles into the five main points.
- Share the top three writing tips you should ever know, etc.

- Revamp other articles – this is not plagiarism. We are notsuggesting that you copy them, but if someone writes an article, you may find that you have an opposing view and reading their article can spark ideas from which to create your own.

Google Chrome have what is called an extension app, which enables you to follow articles written in certain newspapers. You can adjust your 'options' so that you can view only the feeds you want to be subscribed to and only receive material that is relevant to you. For example, if you are interested in articles connected with books, check the box labelled 'books' under 'culture'. Whenever an article is posted online by whatever newspaper it is that you have signed up for, it will show up in a little box at the top of your screen on your toolbar.

Every time a new article is posted in your specific newsfeed, it will notify you by keeping a running tally of the total number of new messages in the top right of your screen until you click 'mark as read'. If they are relevant to your subject of interest or genre, you could repost them for your own viewers. With luck, they will then share your interesting posts with their fans. This is a good way of getting content to go viral, albeit other people's.

Whenever you post or share one of these third-party articles to one of your social media platforms, you will be given the opportunity to make a personal comment and the link opens with a sample of the text and what is known as a thumbnail. You can choose whether or not you want to include this thumbnail, choose another image or leave it blank.

Libel and Slander

Libel is a defamatory or malicious statement in print about a person. It is important to avoid making libellous and slanderous comments even when writing articles or stories. When writing about living people, make sure you do not write anything that can be construed as offensive, derogatory or untrue. The defences against libel are:

- justification (what you said is true);
- fair comment (if the matter is deemed to be of public interest), and
- privilege (covering politics, local government, etc.).

In legal terms, a statement is defamatory (libellous) if it:

- lowers a person's reputation in the estimation of right- thinking members of society (ordinary, everyday people)
- causes a person to be shunned or avoided
- exposes a person to hatred, ridicule or contempt
- disparages a person in their office, trade or profession.

The libelled person must generally still be alive; although 'criminal libel' can apply to the dead. There is no protection if you libel someone by innuendo, sly digs or inferences. You don't have to name someone to identify them; as long as you can tell who you mean, you will be deemed to have identified the individual. And remember that anyone who repeats a libel is liable.

Bias

Bias is a form of prejudice in favour of or against one thing, person or group compared with another, usually considered to be unfair. Keep an eye out for bias, e.g. he/she and his/her. When writing your articles or stories, try rewording to 'one', 'they' or 'you', or replace with a general term for a group/individual, e.g. 'customer'. Alternatives you might consider are:

man	people, we, human beings, person
man	to staff
mankind	the human race
man-hours	work-hours
man-made fibre	artificial or synthetic fibre
policeman/woman	police officer
manpower	human resources, workforce, staff

Copyright

This is the exclusive right to use an original work. Copyright is usually owned by the creator of the original work until they sell or assign it to another party.

You will need to seek copyright if you intend to quote an original work, if the originator of the work died less than seventy years ago from the date of publication. To be more precise, copyright lasts for seventy years from the end of the year in which the originator of the work died.

After that time, copyright becomes public domain and it no longer needs to be sought.

> **Coaching Tip:**
>
> If you find yourself tempted to copy another person's work, ask yourself why you want to do that. If it is because you do not believe in your own talent, then simply practise writing articles. If you believe that copying their work is a quick route to fame, success and money, perhaps you should ask yourself why you want to become a writer.
>
> You should be writing because you love writing and want others to read your work. In our case it is to help other writers. If it is fame and attention you are seeking – that is fine, but there are easier ways to achieve this. You could apply to appear on a reality TV show, for example, which constantly push ordinary people into the spotlight for a short period of time – but even then most disappear back into obscurity, because for the majority of people talent is what counts.
>
> ☺ But not always – there are a few celebrities who hold the nation's interest for things other than talent. However, while I fail to understand why people would want to appear on a show to display their private life to all and sundry, there is no denying that millions of people find it gripping to watch.

If you copy another's work without permission, you are in breach of copyright and can be sued. You can quote from another's work if reviewing it and it is accepted practice to quote a brief passage for general use, provided you acknowledge the source. Sometimes a small fee will be required to obtain the necessary copyright, but it is always a good idea to obtain these rights well in advance of trying to get your work published. This is because it can be a lengthy process and you may not even get a response. We would suggest that you seek copyright permission from the moment you intend to use an external source, even while you are still writing the manuscript – we kid you not!

Images

When using images on the Internet, and indeed in all walks of life, don't be tempted to go on sites such as Google and simply copy and paste images – or at least not if you don't want to wind up in trouble. Many companies that sell images put a tracker on the image and if you copy it and include it on your website, they will be able to detect it through a system which operates by searching the Internet to trace images that haven't been paid for.

Either obtain royalty-free images, pay for the use of an image that you want or take your own. Failing that, you could always employ the services of an illustrator or graphic designer. Try your local college or university – there is lots of young talent available at a reasonable cost.

Permissions

When seeking copyright permissions, you will need to contact the author or publisher direct. The important thing to remember is to provide as much information as possible. The type of information they will be looking for includes:

- wording to be used
- purpose for use
- whether it is to be an Internet-based thing or produced as a book
- how many copies you propose to sell and at what price
- intended market.

Plagiarism

This is when someone presents another author's ideas or writing as their own, including quoting directly from another's work without acknowledging the original authorship. When conducting research and adopting styles from various authors in order to make one for yourself, and by using other resources such as articles, etc., by this we do not mean that you should commit plagiarism. However, reworking an idea and adding your own research, thoughts or wording to describe it is not plagiarism, as in this case you are not pretending that someone else's work is your own.

☺ As we have said before, your primary reason for writing should be your passion for it – so with this in mind we know you won't be a plagiarist by the very fact you are reading this guide, showing your dedication.

Coaching Tip:

Celebrate your successes. Writing your novel can take months, if not years. It can be difficult to remain motivated when you are not receiving any feedback or reassurance of its success, so you need to create your own feedback and successes. If you set yourself a target of following a certain number of fans or to write an article or blog, when you have completed it, give yourself a treat: chocolate, a relaxing bath, a night out with your friends or family – whatever it is, enjoy it. ☺

Summary

Blogging and writing articles can be both enjoyable and fun. For works of fiction, you can write articles on the writing process, setting your scenes, developing characters, achievements, milestones, etc.

Using the information in your non-fiction, self-help or how-to book for articles and blogs allows you to give great free information to potential readers and buyers of your other products and services, which is generally regarded as one of the best ways to get people interested in your work. It also allows you to show people that you know what you are talking about.

Key Points

- Recycle old material after a period of time.
- Only use images that you own and ensure you own the copyright of anything you post.
- Start a notebook of ideas you can use for blogs, articles and stories.
- Don't duplicate content.

- Avoid spamming and overly promoting.
- Remain on topic.
- Choose something current to write about.
- Respond to comments quickly and professionally.
- Include links to your social media platforms.
- Consider using images, slide presentations, videos and photographs, in addition to text.
- Blog at regular intervals.
- Mention your subject as often as possible.
- Ensure you complete your meta description.
- Facts and figures should be accurate.
- Avoid libel, slander, bias and plagiarism.
- Secure permissions in advance.
- Accept the fact that negative comments are inevitable.
- Highlight keywords three times in italics, bold and then underline.
- Welcome and actively encourage feedback; perhaps even send out a feedback form.

Next Steps

- Look at some blogging sites on your topic and see what other bloggers are saying.
- Subscribe to some e-zine sites and have a look at the quality of other articles.
- List ideas for fifty-two blogs or articles (if you can only come up with twelve, don't despair – you can always blog once a month and you will generally find that other ideas will come to you once you get started or read something that intrigues you).
- Consider how you are going to set up your blog.
- Start thinking about the type of content you are going to blog about.
- Consider becoming a guest blogger.
- Choose article titles carefully.

- Comment on other blogs.
- Decide what platforms you want to appear on and where your potential readers might come from.
- Consider writing some short stories.

Chapter Eight – Other Marketing Techniques and Tools

It's not enough that we do our best; sometimes we have to do what's required.

Sir Winston Churchill

Introduction

Although there is no disputing the power of the Internet, it is not the only way to make an impact and market your book. Social media is only one aspect of book marketing. Although not sufficient on their own, traditional tried-and-tested methods are still valid and should not be overlooked.

Marketing Basics

The premise of marketing is to:

- understand your market
- listen to what your audience wants
- engage with your audience, thereby building loyalty and trust
- offer your book and goods/services for sale – never push them at people.
- monitor progress and make changes as and when necessary so that you stay on target
- set yourself objectives and plan effectively.

There is no doubt that getting your book title into shops is a challenge, but it is not impossible – it just takes a little imagination and determination.

The aim of marketing is to know and understand the customer so well the product or service fits him and sells itself.

Peter F. Drucker

Making the Most of Marketing Strategies & Sales Opportunities

There are plenty of marketing opportunities out there and you should make the most of every one available. Take advantage of any sales avenues that you can and depending on the subject matter of your book, you could try some of the following techniques:

- Local press releases and book signings.
- Contact your local radio station/s to see if they are interested in conducting an interview.
- Attend festivals, exhibitions, trade shows, conferences, conventions and book fairs.
- Write an article for local parish magazines.
- Visit hospices, care homes and schools to give talks or readings.
- Appear on TV shows such as ITV's *Loose Women*, BBC's *Breakfast*, ITV1's *Lorraine*, ITV's *Daybreak*, etc.
- See if any local shops or post offices will support local authors and stock copies of your book for a commission.
- Write a press release for a national magazine.
- Consider submitting your book to competitions and enter it for awards, to increase exposure and credibility, as well as gain potential for sales and testimonials.
- Make the most of awards received by publicising it at every opportunity through your business card, in your email signature, on letter-headed paper, on flyers, through social media, on your website, within your book or by using stickers.
- Write short stories for parish magazines.
- If you don't win a competition or an award, you can always stress the fact that you were nominated.

- Contact local schools, colleges and universities to see if they can support you in any way.
- Offer discounts or free giveaways for a limited period.
- Join local literary circles, book clubs and groups such as WIRE (Women In Rural Enterprise), Shropshire Chamber of Commerce, writing groups, etc., who usually hold meetings once a month; there is invariably a membership fee.
- Contact groups, clubs and organisations to become a guest speaker.
- Get your local library or bookshops involved by hosting talks.
- If you have written a non-fiction book, contact groups and organisations specialising in your topic.

When the opportunity presents itself for you to promote your book you need to be prepared. Create a short PowerPoint presentation or slide show to help you deliver your message. This will also come in handy when approaching bookshops to discuss signings and also with other venues for talks. People will take you much more seriously and be more receptive to your requests using this method of approach.

Libraries actively encourage local authors, so consider leaving samples of your book with a review form, file or notebook, to enable people to leave feedback or readers' comments. Many local bookshops are struggling, but one thing they can offer that online retail is unable to do is to hold book signings and launches. Offer to do one for them or perhaps give a talk. Set up a display of your book, allowing retailers to take the books on sale or return, reducing their risk and showing your own confidence in your book.

Creating a Display

If you have the opportunity to create a display of your books either in a shop, at a fair or other event, make sure you are creative. Today, Ladybird books are recognised and loved the world over. In the early days, however, they ensured they caught the reader's attention with eye-catching displays. It does not have to be expensive, but imagination and creativity are a must.

Sourcing Marketing/Promotional Material

Much of your online marketing will be free or at little cost, but you may want to consider investing in getting some of the following printed: posters, flyers, press releases, advance press releases, business cards (ideally with your website URL printed on the front), 4x6 cards, 2x8 banners and a stand-up sign for book signings. You could always buy pens to pass out or send postcards of a picture of your front cover to potential buyers. Bookmarks and stickers are also relatively cheap to produce. You could even have T-shirts designed of one or some of the characters in your book/s. Badges can be another popular choice and can even become collectibles, as can figurines, silicone wristbands and trading cards. Consider the age of your target audience and make a decision based on this.

A good example of someone who has done this effectively is the author of *The Sugar Monsters*, Darren Cockle, who wrote a children's book on the damage that sweets and sugar can do to teeth. As part of his presentations, he organised a goody bag containing a toothbrush, toothpaste, stickers, etc., to give away with a copy of the book, for direct sales to the public. He also gave away fifty-two copies of his book to Hampshire County libraries, with a sticker in the cover directing readers to his website, in addition to doing talks in various schools.

Bookplates, otherwise known as *ex libris*, can personalise individual copies of a book and are a good marketing tool. Bookplates are decorative labels or small prints pasted into the front of the book bearing the author's name or signature. Where they used to indicate ownership of a book, they are now increasingly being used so authors can sign a book or to add a personalised message as a gift for someone.

Preparing for Public Speaking

The thought of speaking to a room full of people fills some people with dread. Ridiculously, more people say they are afraid of public speaking than death – perspective needed here, people! ☺

Far worse than having to give a talk is having to self-promote. Not many of us can stand up and say 'Read my book; it's really great,' without feeling uncomfortable.

> *There are two types of speakers: those who get nervous and those who are liars.*
>
> *Mark Twain*

Don't Expect Perfection

We all know that no one is perfect. Yet when it comes to public speaking, some of us expect to give a speech worthy of Martin Luther King. We magnify every little imperfection and disregard anything we do right. Even the most experienced speakers make mistakes – the difference is that they don't fall apart about it. They carry on with poise, knowing that as most people have no idea what the speaker was intending to say, it is unlikely anyone will notice.

> *Strive for excellence, not perfection.*
>
> H. Jackson Brown Jr.

Accept Your Nervousness

Some of the best speakers in the world still feel nervous before they get on stage. Nervousness is our adrenaline flowing. Successful speakers know how to make this energy work in their favour. In fact, it is often energy that gives them the edge they need to perform at their best. So when you begin to feel nervous, instead of panicking, be glad of the feeling and use it to your advantage.

I have been a fan of the rock legend Bruce Springsteen since I was a teenager. He once observed that he regards his nervousness before a concert as excitement. He knows how to channel these feelings into this performance and having seen him live, I can vouch for the fact that his live concerts are incredible.

Avoid Trying to be Word Perfect

When you are giving a talk there is no need to be word perfect. Attempting to do so will increase any nervousness and stress, and may make you fall apart completely if you realise you have made a mistake. Avoid reading your presentation from a script – to do so runs the risk of the audience tuning out. Speaking is about engaging with the audience and making eye contact, and you can't do that if your focus is on a card in your hand.

Keep it in Perspective

You will have lots of skills, talents and qualities. Never lose sight of the fact that whether you are good at public speaking or not, it is not a reflection of your value as a person. It is just a skill like many others that you can learn and become better at with practice.

The more I practice, the luckier I get.
                                    Gary Player

I am a naturally shy person and at one time if I was asked to speak in front of even a handful of people, I would not have slept for days beforehand and then would have spent days after going over what I did wrong. Now, I am far more relaxed about speaking in front of people, regardless of how many there are. I never write out more than a few headings to topics I want to cover and I simply remember to be me. If you feel unable to consider public speaking or appearing on television, consider other areas where you can market your work, such as radio, printed matter or the Internet.

If you are contemplating appearing on the radio, you will need to consider which show, broadcast or presenter your target audience will be listening to and approach the show's producer. You are unlikely to be successful if you approach them and ask them to interview you about your book. Instead, focus your approach on what you can talk about. If possible, make it topical with what is currently happening in the news. For example, if your book is about how to be happy without a partner, you could approach radio stations to suggest a Valentine's Day phone-in session for those without a loved one. Remember to arrange it in advance about two to three weeks beforehand.

Radio interviews and book signings are effective ways to market your book and while some of you will love the idea of appearing on the TV or radio, and actually desire celebrity status, others will prefer to stay out of the limelight. Incidentally, to state the obvious, radio interviews are easier to secure than TV appearances. If you do manage to secure an interview, the following guidelines may help:

- Avoid 'ums' and 'ers'.
- Use bullet points as prompts.
- Project your voice.
- Don't rush your words out just to get finished.
- Maintain eye contact.
- Check your body language.
- Tell readers how they can benefit from your book.
- Back this up with evidence if possible.
- Dress accordingly – consider the type of audience you are addressing.

- Choose your words carefully and avoid jargon unless appropriate.
- Don't read out from a sheet word for word.
- Take a list of topics you can discuss.
- Always invite questions at the end.

☺ If you are nervous that you won't know the answer, what were you doing writing a book on the subject? Only kidding – just be honest and explain you don't know. Even the most knowledgeable people don't know everything.

Preparing a Press Release

Begin your press release with a simple statement or question, otherwise known as a hook, that will grab the attention of your audience. Focus on what makes you and your book unique and important to readers.

The press release should be a page in length, double-spaced and written in a way that is interesting and informative. You could also use short block paragraphs and bullet points. Limit yourself to seven or eight paragraphs, so that the total content spans just one A4 page. Encourage the recipient to take action to buy your book. Always write in the third person, include a quote, perhaps a photograph.

Your title needs to create impact to attract exposure and it needs to deliver high-quality content. The most effective way is to ensure it is at least one of the following – preferably more:

- Relevant to the audience
- Newsworthy
- Controversial
- Ties in with a current event
- Links to a celebrity
- Has a strong human interest angle

You could also consider some of the following:
- Does it tie in with an event, season or public holiday?
- Is there a national awareness/appreciation day or month it could coincide with, such as National Day on Writing, Family Literacy Day, Love Your Liver, Hug Day, Winnie

The Pooh Day, Thinking Day, World Downs Syndrome Day, Human Rights Day, etc.
- Is there a day it could be released near, e.g. Mother's Day, Grandparents' Day, a special saint's day?
- Does it contain life-altering information?
- Are you motivating or inspiring anyone with ideas or examples?
- Is it current and interesting?

The ideal day to issue a press release is on a Tuesday, Wednesday or Thursday. This is because a Monday tends to be the busiest news day when people are bogged down with paperwork and emails received over the weekend. Fridays tend to be slow days, with people starting their weekend early; if not in body then in mind.

It is best to send your press releases out early in the day. The optimum time would be around 11.00 a.m., because by this time people will have addressed all their other mail and so it will stand out more, giving it more chance of being read. First thing in the morning at around 9.00 a.m., people are invariably busy structuring their day and responding to all their emails from overnight.

At lunchtime people tend to switch off, so it is best to avoid this time. Late afternoon and early evening people are winding up for the day or commuting home. That said, when people are commuting, if they are using public transport, they may be checking their emails and catching up. If your readership is based abroad, you will need to consider the time zone of the country in question.

You should aim to publish one press release a month, to refresh people's memories that you are still there. Engagement rates are believed to be higher on Thursdays, Fridays and weekends, with various studies securing different results. If you post your content at quieter times, while there may be fewer people to view your posts, there is also less competition to get your post noticed above the noise.[1]

Know your market and adapt your style to your chosen market. You will be familiar from reading different newspapers that the writers of these newspapers use different styles for the benefit of their own readership.

The Telegraph and *The Times*, for instance, capture a different audience to that of *The Sun* and *The Daily Mail*. Purchase a couple of different papers and compare how they report the same event or subject matter. See if you can spot any differences, such as the type of language and style they have used. Notice how the sentences and paragraphs vary in length and how the language used differs.

Compiling a Press Release

The best types of press release answer questions such as:

- Who?
- What?
- Where?
- When?
- Why?
- How?

Always write for your target audience when writing a press release and write about things that matter to them. Ensure you use niche words that stand out. A press release comprises the following:

1. Headline – short and to the point; attention-grabbing. Fed up with …? Want to know more about …? Insomnia sufferers – help at last! 100s of ways to … Self-help for chocolate lovers … Technophobes – you will love this book on … Everything you need to know in one book. Ten easy steps … Don't miss out on … Secrets of a XXX revealed!

2. First paragraph – expanding on the headline, this part of the press release stands alone, enthuses and motivates; otherwise known as a lead paragraph.

3. Body copy – the main part containing supportive information on what you are doing, why people should care, quotations by from authority figures, etc. Write an overview then expand on it, leaving smaller details until last.

4. Boilerplate – overview about your company to help people understand what your company does, its location and when it was founded, with details of your products and services. Remember to add details of any awards or accolades you have won. In other words, you boil it down.

5. Contact information.

6. Editors' notes.

You could also include testimonials and endorsements. Avoid overuse of exclamation marks and always check your article for typos and accuracy of facts. The most obvious advice is to ensure you mark the press release for the attention of the right person, so your efforts aren't wasted.

Scribd

Scribd is a document-sharing website that enables users to post material in various formats such as Word, Excel spreadsheets, text documents, JPEGs, PDFs, PowerPoint, etc. However, users need to be mindful that they need to own the copyright, prior to posting any material.

Founded by Trip Adler, Tikhon Bernstam and Jared Friedman in 2006, Scribd is a self-publishing platform where people can publish articles and share files. By sharing excerpts from your book, you can hopefully attract enough interest from readers so they will buy it, thereby increasing your exposure.

The advantage of Scribd is that you can upload an unlimited number of documents and presentations, and you can see who is viewing your files, where they live and how they found it. While it is largely free, in 2013 they launched a paid book subscription service, enabling readers to read books on the Apple and Android devices, in addition to Web browsers.[2]

Advantages of Promoting Your Work on Scribd

- People can ascertain if they want to buy your book by viewing samples.
- If you have a blog, you can link to the extract you have uploaded on Scribd.
- Scribd is easy to use and it is simple to upload material.
- When readers find an author/publisher they like, they can subscribe to their material.
- Readers can print PDF downloads of anything you have uploaded.
- Your subscribers will be able to view new content that you upload.
- Subscribers can rate a document.
- You can post the URL to your excerpt/book on Scribd to your other social media platforms.

If the quality of the material you upload is poor, it may have a detrimental effect on both your reputation and sales – so the first rule should be that you only post material of the highest standard. Don't forget: less is more – so beware of posting too much. If the reader has all the information they need, they will not be motivated to buy your book. Conversely, posting too little means your reader remains unconvinced as to whether or not your book is for them. Getting the balance right takes practice, so experiment.

Opening a Scribd account

To get started:

- Go to <http://www.Scribd.com>.
- Click the 'Login' button to the top right of your screen.
- Click the 'New to Scribd? Sign up for a free account' button.
- Click the 'Sign-Up Now' button on the home page.
- You will be taken to the login screen.
- Create a username (consider using your real name or company name) then fill out your password and email address.
- You will be directed to a home page, which tells you what's been done lately on Scribd, as well as what you've done in the past. It also alerts you to where you need to go to upload documents.
- Click on the top link that says 'Get started by uploading some documents for the world to see'.
- You will be taken to another screen.
- Click the 'upload' button and choose the file you want to upload. Remember, it is the whole file you will upload, so if you only want to upload a sample page/chapter, you will need to save this chapter as a separate file in its own right.
- Enter a title that best reflects your document contents and the subject matter.
- Do the same thing in your description, remembering that it is a social site.
- Tag it with keywords and phrases.

- Don't mark it as private, unless you don't want it to be viewed.
- You can create 'collections' where you have several excerpts from one book collection.
- Choose a category.
- Click 'Publish'.

Make sure you complete your profile. To do this, click on 'View' or edit your profile at the bottom of the screen after you have uploaded your first document. When you have uploaded your photograph, follow the link to go back and edit your profile, where you can fill in details such as hobbies, occupation, etc. You can also add a link to your website.

To give you an idea what you should put, our Scribd profile looks as follows:

Username: MyGuideBookSeries
Name: My Guide
UK Bio:

Publishers of the award winning *My Guide* series of self-help, wellness, health and how-to books, designed to improve lives.

Currently expanding the series and accepting submissions from experienced professionals, coaches, trainers, therapists and thought leaders wishing to write for the series. Writing a book can be the key to enhancing your standing in the professional world, helping you achieve greater success and improving your credibility:

- Establish yourself as an authority figure and an expert in your field
- Share your knowledge with a wider audience
- Open doors to new opportunities, increased business and speaking engagements
- Promote your business and command higher fees
- Create a legacy to your life's work and obtain celebrity status

- Gain the recognition your knowledge, expertise and skills deserve

The team:

- Wellness coach
- Master Practitioner of NLP, Time Line Therapy® & hypnosis
- NLP Coach
- Life Coach
- Meditation Teacher
- Qualified, experienced proofreader & editor
- Award-winning published authors of several self-help books

Interests:

Reading, writing, gardening, walking, dancing (salsa, merengue, bachata, rueda)

Location: Shropshire, UK

Website: <http://www.personalheights.com>

We have also uploaded an image or avatar of our company logo.

GoodReads

Now acquired by Amazon, GoodReads was launched in 2007 and reached 40 million members by 2015, with over 47 million reviews. To give you an idea of statistics, GoodReads members added more than 1.3 billion books to their shelves in 2015.[3] It is the largest site for readers and book recommendations in the world that enables the sharing of books.

It can be incredibly tough for first-time authors to get their book noticed and meet other authors and readers, but GoodReads can offer a solution to this and they also list self-published books. It is a great way to help readers discover your books.

You can request to upgrade your account to Author Program status, entitling you to greater access to all readers on this platform. It also enables you to upload your book titles and add a cover image, a description of your book, an ISBN number, etc. Editing and updating your own book data is easy and you can also list new publications. As long as your author name matches the book exactly, it will appear in your list of published works.

On your GoodReads profile, you need to add a picture of yourself and an author biography. Note that once you have added an author profile, you will then have to complete a second profile, which will be the one visible to readers. You can then:

- Share/upload excerpts from your book/s and other writing.
- Add a link to your personal website or blog.
- Run a Q&A.
- Participate in discussions.
- Create a blog.
- Track and discuss what you are currently reading.
- List a book giveaway, which are free to set up, other than the cost of postage when you mail the book out to the winner. GoodReads also promote giveaways for you.
- Obtain reviews once the book is in circulation and perhaps attract the attention of bloggers, thereby spreading the word of your book.
- Publicise upcoming events.
- Claim book titles you have written; GoodReads will need to confirm that you are the author.
- Maintain a to-read list on one of your shelves.
- Find or make book recommendations.
- Start a group of your own.
- Become a fan of other people.
- Follow other people in your newsfeed.
- Promote your books.

To find groups, search for keywords. Always read individual group rules before contributing to any discussions.

To sign up for an account, go to the GoodReads website at <http://www.goodreads.com/user/new>, enter your name and email

Chapter Eight – Other Marketing Techniques and Tools

address and then assign a password before clicking the 'Sign up' button. Alternatively, you can sign in using Facebook.

To give you an idea what information to include on your author bio if you sign up for the Author Program, we have included the details from our page:

First Name:	Claire
Last Name:	Pickering
User Name:	(customize your URL – Goodreads.com/ClairePickering) ClairePickering
Gender:	Female
Zip Code (US only):	[left this blank as we are in the UK]
City:	Oswestry
State/Province Code:	Shropshire
Country:	United Kingdom
Location Viewable By:	[we selected 'everyone']
Date of Birth:	[we left this blank]
Age & Birthday Privacy:	Age to no one & birthday to friends
Web Site:	<http://www.personalheights.com>

We have also uploaded an image or avatar of our My Guide series logo.

Interests:
Reading, writing, gardening, walking, salsa dancing

What Kind of Books Do You Like to Read?
historical romance, self-help

About Me:
An accredited coach, meditation teacher, NLP master coach, Time Line Therapy® and hypnosis, Claire supports people in taking action so they can make positive changes in their lives and reach their own personal heights. Together with Rebecca, Claire co-developed the award-winning My Guide series of self-help, wellness and how-to books designed

to improve lives. A published author and qualified proofreader and editor, she takes pride in helping authors achieve their goals, demonstrating expertise in editing, publishing and marketing methods that work.

Mission:
- Helping people to improve their lives though a comprehensive range of how-to books.
- Assisting novelists to bring pleasure to others by writing, publishing and selling their novels.
- Supporting people in achieving their own personal heights.

The Importance of Book Reviews

By now you will know that it is important for an author to be noticed and reviews is one way to give you social proof. You have written your book because you want it to be read and obtaining reviews is one way to do this.

With today's vast Internet usage there are a huge number of websites that offer book reviews and it is a good idea to get as many reviews as you can. When submitting to review sites, you need to bear in mind that they will be flooded with submissions, so you need to be patient. In order to establish a relationship in the first instance, always approach them direct before sending off your submission for review. Some review sites require payment for such a service. Reviews can be effective on Amazon and it is a great way of building up recommendations.

Most people read reviews before buying a product. If you are renting a DVD you will invariably read the review first before downloading or ordering a copy. The same applies to books and those of J. K. Rowling's manuscript *The Casual Vacancy* are certainly polarised, with many people objecting to the price, tone, length or message of the story. But we would encourage people to make their own mind up after reading the full book. Let us be clear – if you are hoping for another *Harry Potter* you will probably be very disappointed, as there is no magic or lovable, comical characters. Neither does it have a feel-good ending. But it is a powerful, well-written, quite poignant book, which has sold millions of copies.

It is the same for every book, in that there are always differing opinions. *The Secret* by Rhonda Byrne sold millions of copies and regularly receives five-star reviews, but also a large number of low ratings. But even negative reviews can be turned into a positive, in that you can invite others to comment.

If you do receive a negative review, remember that it is only one person's opinion. We all have different tastes and if you are someone like J. K. Rowling, who is already incredibly successful, she probably isn't too worried about the odd negative review. After all, would you be if you had made millions? And if you had made millions, then surely you would have proved that it was successful, despite what some might think.

To give you an idea of the type of columns you should have in a professional review request document, see below:

- book title
- author name/s
- book cover image
- genre
- word count
- blurb
- brief synopsis

You can also include your banner or logo at the top and a signature, if you have one.

Even though you are only requesting reviews, it is important that your submission looks professional in every sense, as if it has come from a professional, established publishing house or agent.

Skype

Skype can be a useful tool for marketing your book in that it allows you to make calls, including international ones, over the Internet completely free of charge. This means that if you make a connection with booksellers or groups that might be interested in your book, you can set up a video conference call with them to discuss marketing ideas.

Released in 2003, Skype enables users to communicate with others across the globe using a webcam, and through instant messaging over the Internet internationally. Calls to other Skype users are free and it enables you to connect with prospective clients, so if you have started to 'chat' to someone on one of your social media platforms, you can move the conversation over to Skype if they show an interest in what you are doing.

Coaching Tip:

We know that in communication, words only represent 7 per cent of communication – 55 per cent is body language and the rest is tonality. So think about the method you are using to engage people and utilise all the elements of communication to your advantage. If you are writing a blog all you really have are the words, so the words that you use have to be chosen far more carefully. It is possible to say something with two different tones of voice and give it two different meanings. Likewise, at a time of email communication and texting, many problems are caused because your words cannot convey a smile.

If 55 per cent of communication is body language, with the exception of YouTube, the other platforms cannot convey your mood as easily. So remember: whenever you write, you may be sat smiling as you write a post or comment, but it may not come across that way to your readers. With this in mind, you need to check your writing by reading it back to yourself, aloud. We like to tell our readers we are smiling by adding a smiley face. ☺

Summary

Marketing, like any other skill, takes practise. Many people think that talent is something someone has to be born with and certainly some people appear to be born with a natural ability to do certain things. Research has shown that approximately 10,000 hours of practice can take anyone from being unskilled in pretty much any field, to being excellent. If the idea of working for this number of hours before you become a marketing genius is off-putting, remember that the reason you are promoting your book is because you have a passion for your work and you want it to be read.

The best thing that can happen is that your book will instantly be a bestseller in 100 countries and you will have had a great time marketing it. The worst case scenario is that it does not become an overnight sensation and may only sell a handful of copies. But if you have enjoyed the process and have learnt more about marketing, social media and writing – possibly discovering some things about yourself that you didn't know, maybe even laying some demons to rest – you can only win in this situation. And who knows, you may even make some firm contacts or friends ...

Key Points

- Actively seek out every available opportunity to bring awareness to your book.
- Keep plugging away at marketing, little by little and often.
- Consider other marketing ideas.
- Traditional, tried-and-tested methods of marketing still have a valid place.
- Marketing is most powerful when you combine traditional and social media marketing together.
- Understand your market.
- Monitor progress and make changes as and when necessary so that you can stay on target.
- Set yourself objectives and plan effectively.
- Discounts and free giveaways should only be offered for a limited period.

Next Steps

- Make a list of topics you could speak about on local radio.
- Write a press release.
- Visit your local bookstore and library to see if you can get them to stock your book or allow you to run a presentation.
- Come up with a list of things you can talk about, other than your book but related to its subject.
- Contact your local radio stations to see if they are open to the idea of interviewing you.
- Get some simple marketing materials printed.

- Find sites where you can list your book for free or allow book sharing in order to promote interest.
- Upload some excerpts of your book to give people a flavour of your work.
- Prepare a PowerPoint presentation as an aid for when hosting talks.
- Attend book fairs, trade shows, conferences, conventions, etc.
- Join literary circles and writing groups.
- Prepare for public speaking.
- Sign up to Scribd and Goodreads.
- Post some excerpts of your book.
- Request reviews.
- Submit your book to competitions and awards.
- Join Skype.

Footnotes

1. See <http://blog.bufferapp.com/best-time-to-tweet-post-to-facebook-send-emails-publish-blogposts> [accessed 23.12.15]
2. See <http://newscorp.com/2013/10/01/scribd-launches-first-global-multi-platform- digital-book-subscription-service/> [accessed 23.12.15]
3. See <https://www.goodreads.com/about/us> [accessed 23.12.15]

Chapter Nine – Distribution Outlets

Learn from yesterday, live for today, hope for tomorrow.

Albert Einstein

Introduction

At some point you are going to need to consider who is going to distribute your books for you and how you are going to make them available. Look at the different channels you can tap into in order to distribute your book and make it available in as many different places, in as many different forms, as possible: Amazon, Apple, Barnes & Noble, Gardners, Waterstones, WHSmiths, etc.

Nielsens

Nielsens is a non-profit organisation that operates a service providing market-leading data services to more than 100 countries worldwide. The only way they make money is through selling ISBN numbers. However, they will also list titles with other people's ISBN numbers free of charge, as they offer a free listing service to the UK book trade.

While Nielsens will add your title to their list with any valid ISBN number, wherever it may have been issued, it doesn't necessarily mean that booksellers such as Waterstones will list your book, as they prefer you to have UK ISBN numbers allocated by Nielsens.

ISBN Numbers

An ISBN number quickly identifies books that have been published internationally and they are geospecific. ISBN is an abbreviation for International Standard Book Number. The purpose of an ISBN is to establish and identify one title or edition of a title from one specific publisher and is unique to that edition, allowing for more efficient marketing of products for booksellers, libraries, universities, wholesalers and distributors. You need to have an ISBN number if you are going to sell your book on Amazon, Play.com, Waterstones, WHS, etc. In order to obtain an ISBN, you need to register as a publisher with Nielsen BookData at <http://www.nielsenbookdata.co.uk>. Once you have got your book listed with them, book buyers and sellers can buy your book, enabling you to get your work out to the book industry.

All you need to do is complete their documentation then pay for a block of ten ISBN numbers (the minimum order quantity) and an initial registration fee. The list of ISBN numbers will be sent via email on an Excel sheet. ISBN numbers cannot be changed once they have been allocated. If you need to change your ISBN number, you will need to retire the old title and reassign your title with another number.

Nielsens PubWeb

This service enables publishers to input new data or edit their own titles so that booksellers are kept up to date. Pubweb is an online editing service only available to publishers and it is here that you register new and existing book titles. With PubWeb, once you have received confirmation of your registration you can:

- Add new title information.
- Amend existing records, etc.

Once your book is ready for publication and you have assigned your own unique ISBN number, you can register your book on <http://www.nielsenbookdata.compubweb/PubLogon> and upload all its details, including cover images, RRP and copyright wording, which is usually found on the preliminary page.

To sign up for an account you will need to register for this service in the first instance by completing a registration form. Go to <http://www.nielsenbookdata.co.uk/controller.php?page=88> and click on the link to 'complete the registration form'. You can then download a form for completion. You will be given the option to purchase the Enhanced Service for Publishers by emailing publisher.services.book@nielsen.com. Once completed, the form should be emailed to pubhelp.book@nielsen.com.

It usually takes about a week for a book to appear on the Internet. The book can then be ordered through Nielsens, after which you can contact booksellers direct to advise them that it is available.

When completing the relevant forms to assign an ISBN number to your book title, the publication date can be left blank, so that you don't put yourself under pressure. If you do decide to include a date, put one two or three months in advance – you can always bring it back. If you do it the other way, people might complain to Amazon, who will be selling your title even though it isn't yet available.

Nielsen BookData enables you to complete a basic record of your title, including:

- ISBN number
- author/s and contributors
- book title
- subject classification (including BIC code)
- publisher and imprint
- UK availability
- UK price
- format product available in
- territorial rights (where the book can be sold)
- UK publication date
- physical properties of the book
- UK distributor

Once a record has been added to their database, Nielsens notify customers, booksellers, publishers and websites about your new title/s, which can take around four to six weeks to be fully listed.

ISBN Numbers for eBooks

ISBN numbers can also be allocated to eBooks. While it is not currently necessary to have them on some platforms, like Kindle and Kobo, it is advisable so that other retailers can also sell the eBook version of your book. EBook ISBN listings with Nielsens will only be listed to publishers. In other words, if you allocate an eBook with an ISBN number, you can only notify Nielsens for them to list the title if you are a publisher.

EBook versions of your book require a unique identifier as well and you will need a separate one for each platform you are intending to publish your eBook with. For example, if you were to publish with Kindle, Nook, Kobo and iBookstore, you would need four separate

ISBN numbers. Because other retailers require an ISBN, it can be advantageous to purchase one of these unique identifiers, enabling you to distribute your book to a much wider market, through all possible channels.

Please note that there is no such thing as an eISBN, so when you are writing your copyright page, it is sufficient to write ISBN plus the 13-digit number. A print book ISBN cannot be reused for the eBook; it has to be allocated a different ISBN number. If you make amendments to the interior of the book other than a few typos and minor amendments, you will need to allocate a new ISBN number.

Barcoding

Once you have your ISBN number, you will need barcoding software to put the ISBN number onto your book cover. The barcode is unique to the ISBN number, which comprises thirteen digits as of January 2007. The purpose of a barcode is to tell the retailer how much the book is going to cost and how many are left in stock in the warehouse. They can also use barcodes to reorder products easily by scanning it.

Barcoding originated in the 1960s and early 1970s and was designed to standardise machine-readable identification of products. Essentially, it is a rectangular block of parallel bars and light/white spaces, arranged in a particular format. Widely used across the globe, if you want to sell to major retailers, you must have a barcode; many even refuse to accept books without one. However, if you only want to sell through Amazon, then a barcode isn't necessary. Printing houses can also organise barcodes for you, invariably for an additional fee.

It is generally expected that barcodes appear in a certain place on a book's cover, invariably located on the bottom right-hand corner of the back cover, beneath the blurb. This standard location is designed to save time when searching the product for a code. There is lots of free software available which will allow you to create barcodes for your book. Always ensure the ISBN number is included on the barcode image.

Gardners Books

Gardners is an Eastbourne-based wholesaler that specialises in distributing books to retailers. As long as your book details are listed on Nielsens then Gardners will list the title.

To register, email buyersnewpublishers@gardners.com and advise them that you have set yourself up as a publisher, have written a book and you want them to consider selling it for you. They will then invite you to send your book to new publisher services at their head office to be assessed. For Gardners to consider your title, you need to:

- be registered with Nielsen BookData as a publisher
- have a valid ISBN number and a visible barcode
- have a UK stockist
- hold a stock of books already printed
- ensure the book is written in English

If your book meets the above criteria, you are entitled to send a sample review copy to:

> Buyers New Publishers
> Buying Office
> Gardners Books
> 1 Whittle Drive
> Eastbourne
> East Sussex BN23 6QH.

Ensure all books sent are clearly marked as samples.

If they decide to stock your book, you will be notified within four weeks; otherwise, you can take it that they aren't going to. Whilst they consider every submission, Gardners won't necessary take on your book if they think it is not commercially viable. They currently stock 500,000 different titles at any one time and each one has to earn its place in their warehouse, with only a small number becoming stock lines. They will only take it on if the book is outstanding, there is a definite market for it and it is of a good enough quality. The vast majority of titles become 'Special Order' lines, in which case they may order book titles in accordance with customer demand. However, they monitor titles regularly and if they see consistent sales for a title, they will reconsider the situation.

If they do accept your title as a stock item, they will invariably take it on a consignment basis, which means you will receive a purchase order and will be required to send them your books on a sale or return basis. At the end of each month, they will tell you how many they have sold and you then invoice them for this amount.[1]

Bear in mind that like Amazon, they will take 60 per cent of the sales price; Gardners retains 40 per cent and booksellers will be able to sell it on for 20 per cent markup, leaving you with 40 per cent. To apply for an account, you will need to go to <http://www.gardners.com> and click the 'contact us' button. This involves completing a form giving details of your title, but you will need a UK ISBN first, which you can obtain from Nielsens.

If your book becomes a special order item it will be available for book retailers to order. However, this doesn't guarantee that Waterstones and WHSmith will order your books. If they decide they want to have your title on their shelves, you will be invited to send your books to each particular store. Waterstones and WHSmith only deal with Gardners, so there is no point contacting Waterstones and WHSmith direct.

Gardners will put your book title in front of other booksellers in the form of a catalogue and sell it on your behalf. This prevents you from having to go out to all the different booksellers yourself. However, retailers receive lists of thousands of books and you will need to convince them to stock your book – better still, you need to try to get them to place your book in a prominent position in store.

Although getting your book into shops is a challenge, you will need to sell your book through multiple income streams. In addition to Amazon and aside from the ones we have already covered, some of the most popular include:

- Other eBook readers, such as iPad, Kobo, Kindle, Apple, Nook, etc.
- Affiliate websites, where they sell products for you in return for a commission.
- Book Depository.
- Bertrams Books.
- Ingram.
- Baker & Taylor (US-based).

Amazon

The first book ever ordered by a customer on Amazon was *Fluid Concepts and Creative Analogies: Computer Models of the Fundamental Mechanisms of Thought* by Douglas Hofstadter. It was purchased by John Wainwright, a famous computer scientist, in April

1995. Amazon officially opened its doors to the public in July of that year and it is one of the fastest-growing retail websites. Although you can now buy almost anything on Amazon, it is still best known for books.

Amazon take 60 per cent of each book sold, leaving you with 40 per cent of the profit. So if a book costs £10, Amazon take £6, leaving you with £4. However, whilst Amazon take a large percentage of your profit, they are also a market leader. And if you hope to achieve significant sales, it is essential your books are listed here. If you have published through a publisher, the amount you receive in royalties will have been agreed as part of your publishing contract and may differ to the figures given here.

The Amazon methodology is to sell a lot of books very cheaply and it is an incredibly sophisticated marketing system. They don't make a profit on all their books and have what are called loss-leaders, whereby they assume that once you have bought one product you will buy something else in the future. As a customer is making a purchase from Amazon, they will also show them other books and products that might be of interest either now or in the future. This is known as upselling. These strategies certainly work in my case, as Amazon is the first place I go to look for most book purchases.

Internal recommendations are done through varied means:

- Customers Who Highlighted This Item Also Highlighted …
- What Other Items Do Customers Buy After Viewing This Item …
- Customers Who Bought This Item Also Bought …
- Continue Shopping: Customers Who Bought Items In Your Recent History Also Bought …

This is otherwise known as 'queuing', as Amazon are 'queuing' you to perform an action. Amazon rewards increased sales with increased placement in the recommendation queues. These rewards are based on hourly, daily, weekly and monthly sales performance.

All authors are eager to get onto the Amazon bestseller list. You control which category your book is listed under, but you still have to generate sales and increased competition makes it increasingly difficult to reach the top. The best way to qualify for a Top 100 list is to choose a category with the least competition, to leverage better exposure. If you are unsure what category to place your book under, have a look at some other authors whose books are similar to yours and see what they have listed their title under.

Amazon Advantage Account

This is where you list yourself as a publisher so that you can actually sell your books. Applying for an account can take a few days, but it is simple to do, in that you follow this link then click the 'apply now' button: <http://www.amazon.com/gp/seller-account/mm-product-page.html?topic=200329780>.[2] You can then start selling your books on Amazon.

With Amazon, you can build your own author page, but you will need to set up an Amazon Advantage account to do this. To open an account, go to <http://www.amazon.co.uk> and sign up to an author page on Amazon. By adding your profile picture and a biography, you can build confidence in what you are selling.

Once your book has been uploaded onto Amazon, they will do the rest and they will email you any orders so that you can fulfil them. Any new orders will appear in the 'Purchase Orders' box on your screen and all you do is ship it out to Amazon.

Another benefit of Amazon is that you can get customer reviews based on star ratings. Under 'product details' in Amazon there is a sales rank so that you can see how well your book is ranking.

Amazon's Author Central

Amazon's Author Central allows you to share more information about yourself with potential readers. As an author it is vital that you set up your profile so that people can find all the books you have written (even using a pseudonym) and get access to your blog. Amazon.com and Amazon.co.uk run separate Author Central programmes, so they will need to be input separately.

Amazon's AuthorPages

When you list your book on Amazon you will be given the option to create an Author Page. The advantage of having an Author Page is that you can put your author bio there, so that if people searching don't know the title of your book but know your author name, they can also search for you by name. All the books you have ever written will be listed here, next to your profile picture and biography.

Author Pages are designed specifically for the author, who is listed as such. Publishers are listed elsewhere as part of the book's description in the section on 'Product Details' for each book. You cannot merge Author Pages for those who write under more than one name. However, you can manage up to three pen names within a single account and you can manage both Author Pages from your current Author Central account.

Author Pages enables you to display essential information about you, the author, including a biography and author photos, in addition to links to your website and feeds to blog posts, Twitter account, videos, events, etc. You can add this information by clicking the 'add' or 'edit' link next to each section.

When you type in the email address linked to your Amazon account, you will be asked 'Are you this author?', with a list of books they think might be yours that the system automatically throws up. When you are prompted, 'Are these your books?' select those that belong to you and answer 'yes'.

If you release more books in the future, you can add them to your bibliography using the 'Add more books' link, visible within your Author Central account in the 'Books' tab, or by clicking the link 'Are we missing a book?'. You can then search for books written by your pen name by title, author or ISBN before clicking 'This is my book'. Once Amazon has verified that you are the author of the book selected, a second/third Author Page will become available for you to maintain.

Where there are two or more contributors to a book title, as long as you are both using the same email address and password, you can use one Author Central account. To switch between account users, select the drop-down menu to the right of the author's name in the line 'Hello, [author's name]' in the top right of your screen. When you select the name you wish to access, you will be taken to the corresponding Author Central dashboard.

Creating an Author Page URL

This is an easy-to-share link to your page on <http://www.amazon.com> that you can use and share to help with your marketing strategy. On the Author Central Profile tab, click 'add link' next to 'Author Page URL'. A URL will be suggested. If you decide to choose one of your own, it must contain at least one character, with a maximum of thirty, and no spaces or special characters such as dashes, full points and underscores. Once you have chosen an appropriate URL, click 'Save' and your Author Page URL will go live in approximately thirty minutes.

Amazon Authorgraph

This is where you can add a personal digital inscription for an eBook, which is sent directly from an author to a reader's digital reading device as a separate document. To date, 100,000 Authorgraphs have been delivered and if you are an author, you can add your books and start sending Authorgraphs to your own readers. Authorgraphs can also be added as your inscription and signature to the cover image of a book. This feature enables you to personalise and customise messages and you can either use a mouse, your finger (if you use a tablet) or print your name in a script font, the latter being less personal.

Authorgraph can also be used to promote books to anyone on your email list that have yet to be released, using Authorgraph Live! to send an Authorgraph for your new books. Once you have listed your book on Amazon, it will be assigned an ASIN (Amazon Standard Identification Number) number, unique to your book. You can then add this new title to Authorgraph.

Search Inside the Book With Amazon

> *Outside of a dog, a book is man's best friend. Inside of a dog it's too dark to read.*
>
> *Groucho Marx.*

This facility enables readers to view sample pages of a book before buying it. It is free to set up and your book will be more likely to appear in search results if this feature is enabled/activated. As long as you hold the copyright and marketing/promotion rights to your book, you can enrol your book for this feature.

Amazon's Listmania!

Listmania! is a marketing tool for authors whereby all Amazon account holders can create a list of their favourite things, including books. As an author, you can create your own Listmania! list or collection of products on any subject and include your own book, along with those of your competition. You can also ask others to create their own lists and add your book title. To qualify for this service, you must first have purchased a product from <http://www.amazon.co.uk>.

To get started:

- Log into Amazon.
- Click on your name.
- Click 'Your account'.
- Go to 'Personalisation'.
- Click 'Your Public Profile' under 'Community'.
- Click 'Edit Your Profile'.
- Click the 'Lists' tab on the 'Contributions' section.
- Click 'Create your first one now' or 'Manage your Listmania Lists'.
- Complete the relevant information – such as the name of your list (you can have more than one), your qualifications, ISBN numbers, comments (max 400 characters) introduction, tags and product – click 'Preview' then 'Publish list' when you are happy with it.

Amazon Ranking

Amazon use algorithms to rank books and products. While no one outside Amazon knows for sure how the algorithms work, as they are top secret, what appears to be true is that:

- Rankings get you noticed.
- It is now more difficult to fake rankings, as your book now has to be in the top 50 books in your category or 2,000 books overall for a sustained period (not just overnight or for a week).
- Keywords and categories increase exposure.
- If you get forty plus reviews and have an overall rating of 4.5, Amazon may start to promote your book.
- Use keywords in your title, subtitle and description carefully. Consider what your potential market might search for; you can use up to seven keywords or keyword strings, with at least 500 words in your description. You can always change them if they aren't working.
- Your keyword should appear two to five times for every 100 words in your description.

- Avoid having too many competing book titles in your chosen category by ensuring your category isn't too broad.
- Categories change, so update them from time to time. See
- <http://www.amazon.com/-/b/?node=1000> for more ideas.

In essence, it appears that Amazon are looking for books that are consistently selling well and getting good reviews.

Kindle

The Kindle is a form of reader for eBooks that uses a system called 'digital platform text'. It is a fast-growing market and it is easy to upload your eBook onto this site once you have an Amazon account. If you are interested in pursuing this route, visit <http://dtp.amazon.com>.

The advantage of eBooks is that there are no printing costs involved, but it will need to be in a certain format. Once you have got an Amazon Advantage Account you can sign into Kindle and upload your file once you have added the 'go to' HTML coding so that readers can go to the start of the book, the contents page or the cover.

You will be given the opportunity to:

- add a new item
- enter product details
- confirm the content is correct
- upload and preview your document
- enter a suggested retail price
- publish!

You can then add a title, description, author/s, publisher, ISBN and keywords to help promote your book.

KDP Select

Kindle Direct Publishing (KDP) is part of Amazon, so where better to join the eBook revolution! Using KDP Select's free promotions is a great way to find new readers and get your book listed in the top of the Amazon charts.

The aim is to gain readers and reviews by giving away your book for free for specific periods (up to five days) known as free days, in every quarter/three-month period. You have the option to group your free days together in one period or split them over the whole period. Remember that when you sign up for this exclusive programme, unless you opt out of this scheme, you will automatically be enrolled for a further ninety days with a further five days of free promotion, so don't forget to uncheck this box if you don't want this to happen.

One of the constraints of the programme is that when you sign up you are committing to having your book available on Kindle exclusively for a certain amount of time, before you can upload it to other platforms. Even if you opt out, the exclusivity period still applies for ninety days/three months.

To maximise interest and create a book buzz during this period, you should register with free eBook promo websites and post about it on the various social media platforms. For a list of free eBook promotion sites, see: <http://freediscountedbooks.com/free-book-promotion-sites/>.[3] You can also register/advertise that your Kindle eBook will be available for free on the following websites, amongst others:

- <http://flurriesofwords.blogspot.com>
- <http://goodkindles.net>
- <http://indie.kindlenationdaily.com>
- <http://goodbooks-toread.com>
- <http://bookhitch.com>
- <http://www.webook.com>

Assuming you achieve several thousand free downloads over the period that you run the promotion, you will see a surge in paid sales volumes over the next couple of weeks as Amazon's recommendation algorithms kick in based on the:

- number and quality of reviews you receive
- price
- daily download volume
- rank
- number of likes
- conversion into sales ratio.

By 'recommendation algorithms', all this means is that your book is listed more often to potential readers in the 'Customers Who Bought This Item Also Bought ...' section. It is important to get as many downloads as you can during this period where your book is available for free in order to increase your reach, grow your audience and move up your ranking on Amazon. Just because your book is downloaded for free doesn't mean it will actually get read, but it is a good way of getting reviews. When offering your book for free, time of year may be a variable you take into consideration.

Summary

Getting your book into bookstores across the world may be challenging and time-consuming, but that should not be a reason to abandon the idea. Our advice is to start with Amazon, which will enable you to get worldwide online distribution quickly and easily. Once you are achieving a reasonable level of sales and good reviews, it will be easier for you to convince book retailers that you have a marketable product. It should also enable you to negotiate favourable terms for them to stock and distribute your book.

Key Points

- Purchase a UK ISBN number if you are marketing your book in this country, to give your book the best chance of success.
- Make full use of the feature 'Search Inside the Book' on Amazon.
- Consider releasing your book as an eBook.
- Change your book's description, keywords and categories periodically.
- Consider keywords and categories carefully.
- Make your book available on as many platforms as possible.
- Secure as many reviews as possible.
- Use a separate ISBN number for each eBook platform.
- There is no such thing as an eISBN.
- Always use a barcode.

Next Steps

- Decide what distribution channels you want to use and contact them.
- Order some ISBN numbers from Nielsens and join PubWeb.
- Sign up to Nielsens PubWeb and list all new book titles using this service.
- Put your book title in front of Gardners by sending them a sample copy for consideration.
- Apply for a Gardners account.
- Ensure you have an Amazon presence.
- Join Amazon Central on <http://www.amazon.com> and <http://www.amazon.co.uk>.
- Create an Amazon Author Page
- Create an Author Page URL.
- Design an Amazon Authorgraph.
- Obtain some Amazon reviews.
- Start creating your own lists on Amazon Listmania!
- Contact Waterstones' Independent Publisher Coordinator via email to list your book.
- Request a Waterstones Trading Application Form.
- Sign up for KDP Select.
- Set up some 'free' days and register with free eBook promo websites.

Footnotes

1. For more information, please see: <http://www.gardners.com/gardners/content/Downloads/Publishers/Publisher_Guide_to_Distribution_and_Wholesale_Services.pdf> [accessed 23.12.15]
2. Accessed 23.12.15
3. Accessed 23.12.15

Chapter Ten – Organisation and Planning

By failing to prepare, you are preparing to fail.
Benjamin Franklin

Introduction

Hopefully by now you have experimented with the various Internet and social media platforms and perhaps have decided which ones you initially want to focus your marketing efforts on. Thankfully, your decision is not set in stone and you both can and should change your mind if something is not working.

> *The greatest danger for most of us is not that our aim is too high and we miss it, but that it is too low and we reach it.*
> *Michalangelo*

As you begin your marketing campaign in earnest, you need to be mindful that marketing a book is a long-term project. Although many of the marketing options we have explained require little or no funding, you will need at least some sort of funding. Therefore, you might need to supplement your income by selling short stories or writing articles for magazines, where they pay for unsolicited work, which will also help with the marketing process by getting your work noticed. As with writing, marketing your work will take a lot of self-discipline and commitment, but with dedication and determination, you will succeed. Eventually, you will find that it becomes a habit.

Goals

When setting any goal it is essential to have a definitive starting point and a clear goal. Setting objectives keeps you on target. To define your starting point, ask yourself questions like:

- How many people know I have written a book?

- How many books do I sell in an average month?
- How many followers do I have on Twitter?
- How many fans do I have on Facebook?
- How many reviews do I have for my book?

Continue asking questions in this way until you have a clear idea of your starting point.

Now you can set goals and targets, start by setting a goal of how many books you would like to sell in the next twelve months. While we would encourage you to be bold and optimistic, you also have to ensure your goal is realistic to you. This is because if you begin with a goal that you don't feel is achievable, unconsciously you will be making it more difficult for yourself. Once your first goal is achieved you can set new, higher, more challenging goals.

Coaching Tip:

Create a positive image in your mind of your book being sold in shops and on the Internet, and appearing on bestseller lists. Create images of yourself receiving large royalty cheques, or perhaps being interviewed on the TV or radio. Give the images as much detail as possible, even imagining what you would see and what sounds you would hear. Make the colours rich and vibrant.

Analyse whether or not these images you have created feel good or unrealistic. This very simple exercise will give you an insight into what you truly believe is possible. If you feel your goal is unachievable, adjust it to one you feel confident and comfortable with.

You may decide to set smaller goals along the way to keep you inspired. So if you have set a goal to sell 500 books in the next year, help yourself achieve this by setting smaller goals for each month. For example, 10 books in the first month, 30 in the next and so on. Do not fall into the trap of just dividing your target by twelve, because as with most things, sales will probably start off slow and grow quicker towards the end of the year. For example, you may set a target to sell just

2 books in the first month, then 10 in the second, 40 in the third, etc., and then 300 in the final month.

You may wish to set additional goals around income and profit. Depending on your personal circumstances and aspirations, you may also have other reasons for selling your book that are equally or even more important to you, in which case you should set additional goals around those reasons.

Planning

If you don't believe in your product, or if you're not consistent and regular in the way you promote it, the odds of succeeding go way down. The primary function of the marketing plan is to ensure that you have the resources and the wherewithal to do what it takes to make your product work.

Jay Levinson

In many areas of life, successful people are renowned for setting goals and then achieving them. Now it is time to set yourself some tasks. The difference between a goal and tasks is that a goal is something you want to achieve, whereas tasks are things you believe you need to do in order to achieve your goal.

In the case of marketing a book, if you set yourself a task to have a certain number of followers on each platform within a certain number of weeks, this may apply unnecessary pressure and frustration. It may even lead to you abandoning your efforts altogether as you become anxious about the fact that it is not working. This is because you are not completely in control of how many 'likes' you achieve on Facebook or how many people follow you back on Twitter. Therefore, remove unnecessary deadlines and targets. Ensure you are focused on your goal and completing tasks that you believe will make the biggest difference to your success.

Better results are achieved by working daily, with regular input, rather than long bouts of activity and nothing in between, as this can mean you lose momentum and motivation. Marketing takes lots of effort and you should devote a certain amount of time, daily, weekly and monthly so that you are at least progressing the business, by doing something small each day.

For instance:

Daily

- Post 3–5 tweets on Twitter.
- Post 3–5 things on your Facebook wall, maybe highlighting the most important.
- Respond to any DMs (direct messages) on all your platforms.
- Respond to other people's posts on Facebook.
- Retweet other people's tweets, using hashtags and links.
- Visit your RSS reader account and comment on other people's articles/blogs. Share good content on your own platforms.
- Contact one library.
- Contact one independent bookshop.

Weekly

- Request a weekly LinkedIn report from each of the groups you have joined and participate in group activity.
- Post/write a new blog and send the link to your blog to your followers on other platforms.
- Write an article for an external article site.
- Check website, blog, Twitter and Facebook statistics and digests to assess your efforts.
- Write a guest blog.
- Check comments left by fans on the different platforms.
- Review brand/name mentions via Google Alerts.
- Check LinkedIn for new recommendation requests so you don't leave potential connections waiting too long.
- If you have started a group of your own, post a weekly comment for discussion.
- Contact two organisations where you might give a talk or reading; for example: radio stations, schools, groups, rest homes, etc.

- Write some endorsements and recommendations for other people.

Monthly

- Post a question on some of the LinkedIn groups or on your company page.
- Review your Twitter account and check your followers by adding, deleting, etc.
- Review Facebook and LinkedIn groups and followers.
- Review your profiles or bios on your social media platforms; improve on them or amend as applicable.
- Upload a new video to YouTube.

When you first wrote your book, the chances are that you started with a plan or outline and a structure – a blue print, if you like. It is the same with marketing. It is essential that you set yourself realistic objectives if you are not to become overwhelmed and structuring a plan will enable you do this. It will also keep you focused and allow you to feel great every time you achieve your daily objectives.

Coaching Tip:

The nineteenth-century economist Wilfred Parato first pointed out the 80/20 rule – now known as The Parato Principle – when he noticed that 80 per cent of the world's wealth was with 20 per cent of the people. Over the years the 80/20 rule has proved true for so many things.

It is so easy when you are first beginning to use social media to become overwhelmed with ideas and feel as though you have to use them all.

- First, make a list of the ideas you have and divide the number by five. For example, if you have twenty ideas your 80/20 number is four.
- Now look at your list.
- If you are only allowed to use four, consider which are the four most powerful and use those.

Follow in the footsteps of Mr Dickens. Charles Dickens understood about marketing and took action to get his work read by as many people as possible. Because few people in Victorian England could afford books, his work was serialised, making it more affordable, which meant even the working classes could become enthralled by the capers of Mr Pickwick. If he were alive today, there is no doubt he would be getting his work out in as many formats as possible, ensuring he had the widest audience. I suspect he would not have missed any opportunity, perhaps even upselling by having T-shirts made of characters, even postcards or posters.

If there are tasks on your list you do not enjoy, deal with them first. Get them out of the way early and then you can concentrate on enjoying the rest of your day. It can be very distracting to have something lurking in the back of your mind that you know has to be done but that you are dreading. Often, the longer you put them off, the worse the tasks seem.

> ☺ As Brian Tracy – the leading authority on the development of human potential and personal effectiveness – would say: eat your biggest, ugliest frog first. Then the rest of the day will not seem so bad.

One thing is sure – the amount of time spent marketing and promoting your book will be reflected in sales. If you are currently employed in some other way, it is still important to set aside time as you would for any other hobby and make a commitment to yourself to develop your marketing skills. Very few people are born with an exceptional talent and even if they are naturally gifted and proficient in this area, there is a direct correlation between the number of hours that anyone puts into developing any talent and the level of expertise that they achieve.

> **Coaching Tip:**
>
> If you are struggling with time management, make a list of everything you have to do in the next day or week. If your list is overwhelming and just wondering how on earth you are going to get through it puts you in a state of panic, breathe …! ☺
>
> Take a look at your list and ask yourself honestly if it will matter if you never do some of them. Consider

how many things on the list you could delegate to somebody else. Would it matter if you delayed it a day or two? Then pick the three most important tasks and deal with those first.

Don't allow yourself to be distracted from what you need to do – remain self-disciplined and resilient. This will help you to become more organised and will add structure your day, so that you get the most out of it without becoming sidetracked.

When people have got things floating around in their head of things to do, most of us will create the illusion that they all have to be done immediately or the whole world will come crashing down. This is rarely the case, thereby causing unnecessary pressure.

Creating a list will also help you see what you have achieved or accomplished each day, which should give you something to smile about.

Declutter Your Environment

Keep your work area tidy. Don't kid yourself that you actually know where everything is and that a mess actually makes you more organised. An untidy workplace can sap your creative energy. By having a place for things and putting them in their place as you have finished with them, you can avoid mass tidying or filing sessions.

The stress caused by clutter can be enormous. Being in a cluttered environment increases anxiety about all the things you need to do, in addition to making all of the tasks more difficult, thereby increasing stress levels.

The fact is that your sense of calmness and control over your environment is vastly improved by order.

☺ Every time you cannot find something, your stress levels can shoot up as you waste valuable time looking.

Hopefully, you will have realised whilst writing your book that it is a business you are creating and not just a hobby. Therefore, you will already have got yourself into the habit of keeping receipts for expenses such as books, equipment, magazines, newspapers, stationery, postage, advertising, etc. This will be important for the accountant and the Inland Revenue service at the end of the financial year when you complete your Tax Return – having made an income of your talent. ☺

Most expenditure can be offset against your income. Your accountant will be able to help you with what you are and are not allowed to claim. Remember, it is a requirement by law that you retain receipts, invoices, etc., for six years. Invest in a simple lever-arch file, some clear plastic wallets and some dividers, and store your receipts as you make the expenditure – don't become an accountant's nightmare (or dream, because they can charge you more) by walking into their office at the end of the year with a carrier bag full of receipts.

> ☺ It is easy to maintain a tidy work area if you operate the 'touch it once' principle – in other words, when you have finished with an item, put it away. Honestly, it will save you loads of time.

When to do Your Marketing

This comes down to a matter of personal preference and there is no right or wrong way. Different methods will suit different people for different reasons. Many people have expressed the view that the early hours of the day work best, when they are more mentally alert, before distractions kick in and before they are disturbed by the phone ringing. Others work best in the middle of the night, when the creative part of the brain becomes inspired and ideas flow naturally, when everyone else has gone to bed and the house is quiet. But if you are hoping to engage on a live forum this may not work, unless you are engaging with people in another time zone. It might be that you prefer to keep to office hours in order to maintain some sort of discipline and structure to your schedule. Experiment to see what works best for you.

My least productive time is just after lunch, when I have a dip, whereas I find myself becoming more productive in the evening. Only you will know what is right for you and it might be that you need to adjust it according to personal circumstances and mental ability. Once you have decided what time of day you are at your most productive and best able to engage with others, we would suggest keeping to this rather than further experimentation, so that it becomes a habit; unless of course you decide to vary it and connect with different audiences in different time zones.

Where to Work

Again, this comes down to personal preference and circumstances. First, you will need a pleasant and comfortable environment in which to work, with no distractions or interruptions. Consider whether you want to face a blank wall or a view from a window; although, this may be something out of your control owing to physical reasons. If you don't have a stunning view to look out on, you could always put a potted plant in the room or install a window box.

Some people prefer a quiet environment in which to work, while others need background noise, music or the TV for inspiration. If you are making phone calls, you should not have any background noise.

> ☺ I have located my office in the middle of the house, towards the front. From this position I have a wonderful view of the countryside, I can see who has turned up on my doorstep ... and I can see what mischief the kids are up to, as they have to get past me before they go into another room or outside. I can also hear what they are watching on TV to check that it is suitable – although this can work in reverse if they become noisy!

Choose where you work carefully and ensure that you are ergonomically positioned, that your chair is comfortable and that you are not sitting in a stooped position or with your shoulders hunched. Take regular breaks from the screen to avoid repetitive strain injury (RSI) or eye strain, which may lead to headaches and all sorts of other complications. Look at your keyboard and mouse positioning. The best position for your screen is at eye-level, directly in front of you, if you are to avoid neck strain. If you already have a medical condition, such as rheumatism or arthritis, this will be especially important.

Perseverance

Don't get disheartened – marketing is a long process that takes perseverance and dedication. Be prepared to research different options. As Frank Sinatra once said: 'The best revenge is massive success'.

> **Coaching Tip:**
>
> We are all prone to worrying about the future, rather than celebrating it, in that we find it easy to imagine that

negative things will become a reality, whereas positive things are unlikely to happen. The best thing is to take on the following mindset:

- I don't know if this marketing strategy will work, but I am going to try it anyway.
- I don't know if this is the correct social media platform for me, but that doesn't matter. I am going to try it for ten weeks whatever happens, just because it seems like fun.

Focus on what you *can* control instead of worrying about the things you can't. Learn from your mistakes and keep an open mind. By adopting this attitude there is no pressure around success. The best outcome is that you will achieve all your goals and enjoy the journey. In the worst case you may not have achieved your objective, but you may have learnt lots of new things, made new friends, opened up new possibilities and found new things you enjoy doing.

☺ Remember some things won't work. But there is no such thing as failure – only feedback. You only really fail when you stop learning.

Done for the Day?

As a writer, if you want to sell your work you are in effect a business and it is very easy to feel that while there is daylight or even electricity, you must be working. But this is a sure-fire way to burn yourself out. So unless you are completely in the flow and really enjoying yourself, set yourself realistic targets each day as described in this chapter and when you have completed your objectives, stop.

Take regular breaks, because the average concentration span dips after ninety minutes and the quality of your work will begin to deteriorate. Taking a short break of just ten to fifteen minutes and doing something else that is completely different, preferably that involves getting some fresh air, will enable you to return refreshed and far more productive.

Coaching Tip:

It is impossible for us to tell you how long to work for each day or to predict how long you can work at using social media marketing techniques each day before the quality of your posts, tweets, sales patter and marketing pitch deteriorates, so here are some pointers as a guideline. Stop and give yourself a break if:

- You have physical discomfort from sitting, etc. – e.g. back or neck pain.
- You are struggling to find content.
- Your mood is changing, you are becoming irritable and you feel like strangling the people you are engaging with through social media. ☺
- Your eyes are beginning to sting from staring at your computer screen.
- You find that you have been repeating yourself.
- You start making mistakes.

If you believe in something, work nights and weekends, it won't feel like work.
Kevin Rose

What Qualifies a Book to Become a Bestseller?

There is no greater agony than bearing an untold story inside you.
Maya Angelou

In everyday use, the term 'bestseller' may be used very loosely, indeed, and is not usually associated with a specified level of sales. Whilst it may be a bestselling book, it does not denote that it is of superior academic value or literary quality – it simply means that it has sold the most copies in a given time period. In fact, there are a number of modern bestsellers that are poorly written but have achieved an incredible volume of sales because of great marketing.

A book becomes a bestseller when it is included on lists of current top-selling or frequently borrowed titles, and is therefore identified as being extremely popular. The lists are published by newspapers, magazines or bookstore chains, and are based on library circulation statistics, the publishing industry and book trade figures. Some lists are broken down into classifications and specialties, such as fiction, non-fiction, children's, young adult, romance, thriller, etc.

One of the best-known bestseller lists for the US and possibly the world is the *New York Times* Best Seller List, which tracks sales from Internet retailers such as Amazon and Barnes & Noble, as well as national and independent bookstores. But there is no magic shortcut that will make your book appear on the bestseller lists and readers don't appear out of nowhere. However, the more places your book is available for sale, the easier it will be for people to discover find it.

> *There are no magic wands, no hidden tricks, and no secret handshakes that can bring you immediate success, but with time, energy and determination you can get there.*
>
> Darren Rowse

Summary

Taking a little time to achieve the right mindset and to ensure you understand what works best for you and your book will in the long run make the marketing process far more enjoyable, more productive and less disappointing.

- ☺ If you have ever attempted even the simplest DIY task, you will already know how much easier it is if you have the correct tools for the job. So don't make life difficult for yourself – 'tool-up' correctly from the outset.

Hopefully by now you will have decided which marketing platforms and techniques you want to use. You will have established how much time you can devote to marketing, investigated your target market and how to engage them. And now – armed with the confidence that your book contains beneficial or thought-provoking information, or is an engaging and enjoyable novel with an appropriate price and great title, cover and blub – you are now ready to sell copies. ☺

Key Points

- Get organised.
- Plan, plan and plan again, so that your time is spent productively and effectively.
- Marketing is a long-term project.
- Deal with tasks you don't enjoy first.
- Remove any unnecessary deadlines or self-imposed pressure around success.
- Ensure that you take regular breaks.
- Manage your time effectively, using time-management techniques if necessary.
- Structure your day and set aside time to market and move your business forward on a daily basis.
- Make sure your working environment is ergonomically friendly.
- Declutter your environment.

Next Steps

- Set yourself realistic and achievable goals and targets with smaller goals along the way to keep you motivated.
- Set yourself some tasks in order to achieve your goals.
- Decide when, where and how much time you can dedicate to marketing.
- Decide which marketing avenues you are going to use.
- Limit yourself to spending a certain amount of time in each area, so that you don't get carried away with just one task.
- Begin your marketing strategy with the end in mind.
- Operate the Parato Principle.

Final Note From the Authors

You have now reached the end of our guide and we hope you have enjoyed the marketing journey as much as we have. It would be almost impossible for you to have taken everything in in one reading. To get the most out of this guide, keep going back to chapters and reviewing the information to ensure you understand it as you begin to learn each platform. Consider highlighting important points that you may want to refer to at a later date. Whenever you release a new title, revisit the contents of this guide to see if you can improve your marketing strategy.

- ☺ There is no failure – only feedback. We only really fail when we stop learning.

- ☺ We wish you success and look forward to seeing your name on the bestsellers lists.

While there are no shortcuts in online marketing, the important thing is to have fun. We look forward hearing your success stories. Until we meet again, if you would like more information on our other self-improvement publications in the My Guide series of self-help, wellness and how-to books, designed to improve people's lives, please visit <http://www.personalheights.com/book-coaching> or <http://cambridge-media-group.com>. Currently accepting submissions from qualified professionals, coaches, trainers, thought leaders and therapists.

Claire & Rebecca

Index

advertising 16, 33, 53, **62–64**, 82, **84**, 122, 134, 141

algorithms 131, 187, 189

Amazon 22, 23, 26, 43, 56, 87, 122, 123, 172, 177, 178, 179, 180, **182–190**, 204

Apple 83, 166, 177, 182

iBookstore 83, 179

apps 48, **55–56**, 64, 80

articles 52, 68, 69, 75, 86, 101, 112, 131, 133, 136, **139–154**, 158, 166, 193, 196

audience **10–11**, **17–19**, 26, 28, 36, 38, **41–42**, 43, 47, 51, 52, **57–59**, 60, 63, 64, 68, 69, 71, 85, 97, 107, 108, 109, 110, 111, 124, 126, 135, 149, 157, 160, 161, 162, 163, 164, 165, 168, 190, 198, 200

authority figure 8, 14, 34, 62, 43, 60, 62, 104, 107, 134, 165, 168, 198

avatars 70, 71, 108, 169, 171

banners 27, 54, 125, 135, 160, 173

barcodes **180**

Barnes & Noble 177, 204

bestseller 8, 9, 43, 88, 183, 194, **203–204**

bias 101, **151**

biographies 40, 170, 184, 185

blogging 52, 60, 62, 74, 78, 83, 84, 87, 94, 101, 123, 126, 128, 132, 133, 134, **139–145**, 146, 166, 170, 174, 184, 185, 196

guest blogging 141, **144–145**, 196

blurbs 8, 27, **28–29**, 109, 173, 180

book

covers 8, 9, **25–29**, 70, 71, 100, 111, 112, 115, 160, 169, 173, 178, 180, 186, 188

signings 56, 59, 82, 85, 128, 158, 159, 160, 162
sellers 96, 173, 177, 178, 179, 182
shops *see* sellers
stores *see* sellers
titles 9, 22, **21–25**, 115
branding ... 9, 13, 25, **33**, 34, 52, 54, 55, 60, 69, 70, 74, 100, 196
business 36, 37, 41, 44, 48, 52, 53, 54, 55, 56, 59, 63, 68, 94, 95, 96, 99, 102, 108, 123, 124, 135, 146, 168, 195, 199, 202
buzz 115, 140, 189
call to action 63, 109
celebrities 7, 8, 60, 67, 70, 121, 152, 162, 163, 168
communication 48, **174**
community 34, 47, 57, 58, 74, 139
competition 10, 19, 20, 21, 117, 126, 128, 129, 158, 164, 183, 186
connection 29, 34, 37, 40, 47, 53, 54, 78, 94, 95, 96, 97, 99, 100, 101, 105, 106, 109, 110, 117, 121, 123, 130, 136, 149, 150, 173, 196, 200
constraints 48, 67, **79–82**, 130, 189

content 9, 10, 11, 14, 19, 20, 25, 26, 34, 36, 38, 52, 58, 60, 62, 64, 69, 73, 74, 78, 79, 80, 82, 84, 97, 106, 114, 116, 121, 123, **125–126**, 130, 131, 132, 133, 134, 135, 142, 143, 144, 145, 147, 150, 163, 164, 166, 167, 168, 196, 203
conversations 33, 36, 41, 48, 63, 68, 73, 75, 78, 82, 83, 97, 98, 106, 174
copyright 106, 110, **114**, 140, 143, **151–153**, 166, 178, 180, 186
customers **17–18**, 20, 36, 79, 95, 123, 127, 141, 183, 184, 189
designers 25, 26, 122, 123, 153
discussions 96, 97, 98, 99, 104, 105, 106, 170, 196
eBooks 21, 25, 83, 128, **179–180**, 182, 186, **188–189**
editing 10, 28, 40, 50, 58, 77, 103, 144, 145, 148, 165, 168, 169, 170, 172, 178
emails ... 9, 19, 37, 48, 49, 56, 60, 78, 104, 105, 110, 115, 128, 130, 158, 164, 174, 186
endorsements 9, **27–28**, **106–107**, 166, 196

engagement 17, 28, 33, 34, 36, 37, 40, 41, 42, 47, 48, 53, **57–59**, 60, 61, 62, 64, 65, 68, 69, 85, 93, 94, 95, 97, 98, 102, 115, 125, 126, 127, 128, 140, 145, 157, 164, 168, 174, 200

excerpts 71, 109, 110, 166, 168, 170

exposure 105, 158, 163, 166, 184, 187

extracts *see* excerpts

Facebook 34, 37, **47–65**, 68, 70, 71, 78, 86, 87, 93, 94, 111, 112, 113, 123, 133, 135, 171

facts and figures 148, 166

fans 48, 49, 52, 54, 57, 58, 59, 60, 61, 64, 68, 69, 79, 80, 85, 94, 115, 127, 136, 150, 154, 194, 196

feedback 16, 36, 154, 159, 202

fiction **10–14**, **21**, **128–129**

followers 9, 19, 34, 37, 41, 42, 52, 53, 56, 60, 62, 64, 68, 71, 72, 74, 75, **77–79**, 80, 81, 82, 83, 84, 85, 88, 102, 112, 116, 141, 194, 195, 196, 197

forums 18, 145, 200

freebies 59, 82, 109, 127, 130, 159, 170, 188

Gardners Books ... 177, **180–182**

giveaways *see* freebies

goal-setting 8, 10, 12, 13, 14, 16, 17, **42–44**, 49, 82, 85, 99, 103, 109, 172, **193–195**, 202

GoodReads **169–172**

Google 23, 95, 102, 123, 129, 130, 131, **133–136**, 143, 144, 146, 150, 153, 196

grammar 64, 99, 126, 142

groups 18, 34, 41, 48, **61–62**, 63, 83, 95, **97–99**, **100**, 112, 135, 139, 151, 159, 170, 173, 196, 197

illustrators *see* designers

interaction *see* engagement

Internet 9, 15, 18, 26, 28, 30, 34, 36, **41**, 55, 95, 111, 121, 153, 157, 162, 172, 173, 178, 193, 194, 204

interviews 8, 82, 110, 158, 162, 194

ISBN numbers 56, 170, **177–180**, 181, 182, 185, 187, 188

keywords ... 57, 63, 71, 73, 74, 75, 78, 83, 86, 95, 97, 102, 104, 110, 124, 125, 126, 129, 131, 132, 133, 134, 143, **146–147**, 167, 170, 187, 188

Kindle .. 179, 182, 187, **188–189**

Kobo 179, 182

language 18, 64, 106, 121, 145, 165, **174**
body language 162, 174
leveraging 36, 42, 60, 183
libel 101, **150–151**
libraries 159, 160, 177, 196, 204
likes 55, 57, 60, 112, 189, 195
limitations *see* constraints
LinkedIn 37, 68, 86, **94–107**, 196, 197
links 56, 57, 58, 60, 62, 63, 68, 69, 73, 74, 75, 78, 81, 82, 83, 84, 86, 87, 98, 101, 108, 112, 114, 122, 123, 126, 127, 129, 134, 135, 142, 143, 144, 145, 150, 155, 163, 166, 170, 185, 196
literary circles 68, 124, 159
logos 26, 55, 70, 100, 105, 126, 169, 171, 173
magazines 8, 18, 28, 111, 117, 145, 158, 193, 199, 204
meta
  description 129, 142
  tags 128, 129, **130–132**, 142
milestones 43, 54
mindset **7–30**, 149, 202
money-back guarantees 127

monikers 41
negativity 11, 22, 34, 140, 146, 173, 202
networking 34, 36, 37, 42, 47, 58, 94, 95, 96, 98, 99, 101, 112, 115
newspapers 8, 18, 69, 145, 150, 164, 195, 204
Nielsens **177–180**, 181, 182
non-fiction .. **8–9, 20–21, 127–128**
novels *see* fiction
opportunities 14, 18, 36, 42, 44, 60, 62, 70, 95, 96, 102, 112, 121, 141, 145, **159–159**, 168, 198
pay-per-click, ... 62, 134
pen names *see* pseudonyms
perseverance **12, 201–202**
phishing 62
Pinterest 37, **111–114**
pixels 54
plagiarism 150, **153–154**
planning 12, **14**, 61, 129, **193–203**
platforms *see* social media
plug-ins 83
positivity 12, 16, 17, 22, 173, **194**, 202
presentations 126, 143, 159, 160, 161, 166

press releases 158, 160, **163–166**
pricing 9, 10, **20–21**, 114, 116, 127, 149, 185
profiles 49, 65, 94, 197
promotions 28, 36, 59, 60, 61, 98, 115, **160**, 188, 189
proofreading *see* editing
pseudonyms 41, 184, 185
public speaking 15, 44, **160–163**, 168
publicity *see* advertising
questions 10, 28, 29–30, 34, 40, 42, 59, 68, 82, 95, 99, 105, 110, 149, 163, 165, 193, 194
ranking 122, 123, 125, 129, 133, 137, 180, 184, **187–188**, 189, 190
reach 9, 33, 36, 55, 57, 64, 68, 69, 99, 135, 141, 190
recommendations 9, 95, 97, 100, **106**, 112, 134, 169, 170, 172, 183, 189, 197, 196
relevance 19, 20, 42, 60, 63, 64, 68, 75, 79, 82, 86, 94, 97, 99, 102, 123, 126, 129, 132, 133, 134, 135, 136, 141, 144, 150, 163
reputation 64, 82, 142, 144, 148, 151, 167

reviews 8, 10, 21, 22, 27, 28, 36, 97, 110, 127, 148, 152, 159, 170, **173**, 184, 187, 188, 189, 190, 194
RSS 84, **132–133**, 196
scheduling 52, 85, **86–88**
Scribd 166–169
search engines 60, 81, 122, 123, **129**, 130, 131, 132, 133, 134, 142, 143, 144, 146, 147
short stories 145, **148–150**, 193
Skype 173–174
social media 11, 14, 15, 20, **30–45**, 49, 52, 53, 60, 67, 68, 70, 77, 78, 85, 88, 93, 94, 95, 98, 99, 109, 101, 111, 112, 115, 123, 132, 133, 135, 139, 142, 145, 150, 155, 157, 158, 166, 169, 173, 174, 175, 179, 189, 193, 195, 196, 197, 202, 203
social networking *see* networking
SocialOomph 78, **85–88**, 130
spam 58, 62, 72, 73, 82, 106, 129, 134, 141
squeeze pages 130
status updates 47, 100, 101
straplines **39**, 116
target audience, *see* audience
testimonials 27, 49, 56, 110, 127, 158, 166

thumbnails 26, 27, 150
time zones 164, 200
time-limited offers 127
title tags *see* meta
topics 8, 10, 14, 39, 40, 41, 53, 58, 59, 60, 61, 68, 69, 71, 73, 77, 82, 84, 86, 94, 98, 101, 109, 110, 127, 129, 135, 136, 139, 141, 143, 145, 148, 149, 159, 162, 163
Twitter 37, 41, 49, 60, **67–89**, 93, 94, 101, 111, 123, 130, 133, 135, 136, 145, 185, 194, 195
  hashtags 71, **73–75**, 85, 89, 135, 196
  unfollowing 79, 80, 81
upselling 14, 19, 128, 145, 183, 198
URLs 49, 62, 86, 89, 108, 122, 124, 130, 131, 132, 136, 160, 166, 171, 185, 186
videos 9, 37, 49, 62, 68, 84, 101, 107–111, 115, 117, 121, 126, 129, 140, 143, 173, 185, 197
visibility 36, 96, 112
Waterstones 177, 178, 182
websites 28, 37, 52, 56, 57, 68, 74, 84, 87, 89, 98, 112, 113, 115, **121–135**, 139, 141, 143, 144, 145, 146, 153, 158, 168, 170, 189, 196

whitelisting 80, 81
WHSmiths 177, 182
word of mouth 8, 9
WordPress 83, 84, 121, 122, 123, 139
YouTube 37, 60, 62, 68, **107–111**, 174, 197

Glossary of Terms

Affiliate: officially attach or connect to an organisation through a link.

Algorithm: step-by-step process or rules followed in calculations or other problem-solving operations, especially by a computer.

App: short for application program or piece of software designed to fulfil a particular purpose.

Avatar: icon or figure representing a particular person. Bio: biography or account of yourself, the author.

Blog: website or web page on which an individual records opinions, and links to other sites, etc., on a regular basis.

Blogger: person who adds new material to or regularly updates a blog. Blogroll: list of hyperlinks (on a blog) to other blogs or websites.

Blurb: short résumé on the back cover of a book that tells the reader what the book is about.

Brand: type of product or person under a particular name. It is primarily something to build, promote, sell, create or develop. As the author, you are the brand.

DM: direct message.

eBook: electronic version of a printed book that can be read on a computer or other handheld device.

Embed: incorporate text or code within the body of a file or document.

Endorsement: where someone validates a book with a short testimonial.

Engage: establish a meaningful contact or connection with someone. ePub: industry standard electronic book format.

Excerpt: short extract from a piece of writing.

Forum: meeting or medium where ideas and views on a particular issue can be exchanged; an Internet message board.

Genre: style or category of art, literature or music, e.g. thriller, science fiction, romance, military, etc.

Hashtag: a word or phrase preceded by a hash (#) sign used to identify messages on a specific topic.

High bounce rate: when an Internet surfer clicks straight out of a site because the content is not relevant to their search.

Home page: the introductory page of a website, typically serving as a table of contents for the site.

Hosting: web pages are hosted on a server that makes website pages visible to the world 24/7.

House style: a company's preferred manner of presentation and layout of written material, used to ensure consistency.

HTML: Hypertext Mark-up Language (formatting instructions).

HTTP: Hypertext Transfer Protocol: technology used to communicate between servers and web users.

ISBN: international standard book number; a unique 13-digit number assigned to every book before publication, recording details such as language, origin and publisher.

ISP: Internet Service Provider.

Jacket: another name for the cover of a book.

Keyword: a word used in an information retrieval system to indicate the content of a document.

Leverage: the power to influence a person or situation.

Logo: symbol or other small design adopted to identify a product or company, typically no bigger than the size of a thumbnail.

Low click-through rate: where a website is listed on a search result but consistently not picked.

Metadata: set of data that describes and gives information about other data.

Meta tag: used to provide information about a web page for search engines and website users.

Moniker: informal name you can be identified by.

Optimise: rearrange or write data, software, etc., to improve efficiency of retrieval or processing.

Pay-per-click: advertising whereby every time someone clicks on a website, the advertiser pays a fee.

Glossary of Terms

Pixel: a minute area of illumination on a display screen – one of many from which an image is composed.

Platform: term used to describe your Internet presence that allows you to be visible to your audience and interact with them.

Plug-in: module or software able to be plugged in or added to a system to give extra features or functions.

Post: announce or publish something; make information available to an Internet message board or blog.

Profile: short article giving a description of a person or organisation.

Ranking: the position (in relation to others) where search engines place your website based on the keywords and phrases used by the Internet user when searching for things on the Internet.

RSS: short for Really Simple Syndication, a standardised system for the distribution of content from an online publisher to Internet users.

Search engine: a program that searches for and identifies items on the Internet that correspond to keywords or characters specified by the user.

SEO: search engine optimization – the process of affecting the visibility of a website or a web page in a search engine's 'natural' or 'unpaid' 'organic' search.

Server: computer designed to process requests and deliver data to other computers over a local network or the Internet.

Social media: websites and applications used for social networking.

Social networking: the use of dedicated websites and applications to communicate with other users or to find people with similar interests to oneself.

Spam: irrelevant or inappropriate messages sent on the Internet to a large number of users.

Synopsis: summary of what the book is about; useful when submitting work to publishers and/or agents.

Tag: a character or set of characters appended to a piece of text or data in order to identify or categorise it.

Testimonial: formal written or spoken statement testifying to someone's character and qualifications.

Thumbnail: where an image is reduced in size to that equivalent to a small thumbnail, almost like the size of a postage stamp.

Timeline: reverse chronological history of all the things you have done.

Traffic: messages or signals transmitted through a communications system.

Upsell: persuade a customer to buy something additional or more expensive, like a product or service.

URL: short for universal/uniform resource locator – the address of a World Wide Web page, e.g. <http://www.personalheights.com>.

Viral: relating to or involving the rapid spread of information about a product or service by viral marketing techniques.

Virtual: in computer terms, not physically existing as such but made to appear to do so by software.

Website: location connected to the Internet that maintains one or more web pages.

Whitelist: opposite of blacklist.

Widget: an application or component of an interface that enables a user to perform a function or access a service.

WordPress: free, web-based software program that anyone can use to build and maintain a website or blog.

About the Authors

Author of several self-help books, Rebecca Richmond has enjoyed a highly successful career within global organisations, later going on to become a coach. Having triumphed over adversity and cancer, as a qualified coach, master practitioner of NLP, hypnosis and Time Line Therapy™, she is ideally equipped to help you achieve the success you deserve as an author.

An accredited coach, meditation teacher, NLP coach and master practitioner of NLP, Time Line Therapy® and hypnosis, Claire supports people in taking action so they can make positive changes in their lives and reach their own personal heights. Together with Rebecca, Claire co-developed the award-winning My Guide series of self-help, wellness and how-to books designed to improve lives. A published author and qualified proofreader and editor, she takes pride in helping authors achieve their goals, demonstrating expertise in editing, publishing and marketing methods that work.

Other Books in the My Guide Series

How to Write a Novel
Manage Chronic Pain
Overcome Insomnia
Manage Fibromyalgia/CFS
Master Stress: Tame Your Inner Monster

Coming Soon:

Grammar Rules!

Understanding Your Human Smoothie

How to Write a Self-Help Book Fast!

www.ingramcontent.com/pod-product-compliance
Lightning Source LLC
Chambersburg PA
CBHW051821090426
42736CB00011B/1588